Praise for *The Curricular Approach to Student Affairs: A Revolutionary Shift for Learning Beyond the Classroom*

"The message at the heart of this pathbreaking book is clear: We cannot truly understand and respond to students as whole people without supporting their learning holistically across the entirety of the college experience. Learning outside the classroom should be as curricular as is the academic experience—not 'cocurricular,' but fully curricular, integrated, and aligned with an institution's academic mission and values. An accidental, situational, or happenstance approach to learning in student affairs (still easy to find) is a wasted opportunity; it fails to deliver on the promise of higher education. Starting with the principle that we must not bifurcate students' experience (academic versus out-of-classroom), these authors guide us capably and carefully toward a curricular approach that preserves the potential of both students and higher education."—**Richard P. Keeling**, *Principal, Keeling & Associates, LLC; and Editor,* Learning Reconsidered

"Too many professional books are written by people with great ideas and who care deeply but who have not lived the work. This book exemplifies the best of the late Lee Knefelkamp's practice-theory-practice model (PTP). These experienced authors have done this hard work, reflected on their experiences to identify principles, created theories and useful models, and pushed that wisdom back into practice on every page. Institutions have a moral imperative to make all students' experiences educationally purposeful. This book takes that quest to new levels of excellence. Even something obvious becomes revolutionary when implemented in practice built on the integrity of years of wise experience."—**Susan R. Komives**, *Professor Emerita, University of Maryland; and Past President, Council for the Advancement of Standards in Higher Education*

"This book will serve as a valuable resource for anyone seeking to provide rigorous, empirical, and theory-based student experiences beyond the classroom. With students from increasingly diverse backgrounds—culturally, socially, technologically, academically—attending college in the 21st century, higher education needs to be prepared to facilitate learning in every aspect of its work, and this book provides a strong foundation for student affairs practitioners."—**Karen Kurotsuchi Inkelas**, *Associate Professor, Curry School of Education; Research Director, Crafting Success for Underrepresented Scientists and Engineers; and Research Director of Undergraduate Initiatives, Contemplative Sciences Center, University of Virginia*

"*The Curricular Approach to Student Affairs: A Revolutionary Shift for Learning Beyond the Classroom* is a ground-breaking text in which the authors deftly describe a comprehensive, student-centered approach for learning outside of the classroom. They detail the rationale behind this approach, use poignant examples to explain how this approach can be implemented, and provide direction to senior student affairs administrators regarding leadership and organizational change. Following the guidance offered in this book will transform how a division of student affairs operates and actualize student learning and development."—**Gavin Henning**, *Professor of Higher Education and Program Director, Master of Higher Education and Doctorate of Education Programs, New England College; and Past-President, Council for the Advancement of Standards in Higher Education*

"Drawing on the expertise of faculty and residence life educators, the curriculum-based approach to student learning constructs a comprehensive goal-directed learning experience for students. This well-researched book provides a detailed guide to developing and implementing this educational approach to advance student learning in residence halls. Residence life educators committed to engaging students in intentional goal-directed learning experiences must read this book."—**Gregory S. Blimling**, *Professor (retired), College Student Affairs Program, Rutgers University Graduate School of Education*

"This book offers an exciting synthesis of over a decade's committed work to improve students' cocurricular learning in a variety of beyond the classroom environments. The systemic and intentional approach is a leading paradigm shift. The passion and dedication of the team delivering this book and the wisdom offered are guaranteed to improve the student affairs work on any campus."—**Adrianna Kezar**, *Dean's Professor of Higher Education Leadership, Director of the Pullias Center, and Director of the Delphi Project on the Changing Faculty and Student Success*

"The curricular approach to student learning and engagement beyond the classroom is a fundamental need for all campus communities. I am excited that my professional colleagues now have a definitive resource to develop sequenced, mission-driven, and scholarship-based initiatives that will ultimately enhance the college student experience."—**Vernon A. Wall**, *Director, Business Development, LeaderShape, Inc.; and President, ACPA–College Student Educators International, 2020–2021*

THE CURRICULAR APPROACH TO
STUDENT AFFAIRS

THE CURRICULAR APPROACH TO STUDENT AFFAIRS

A Revolutionary Shift for Learning Beyond the Classroom

Kathleen G. Kerr, Keith E. Edwards, James Tweedy, Hilary L. Lichterman, and Amanda R. Knerr

Foreword by Stephen John Quaye

NEW YORK AND LONDON

First published 2020 by Stylus Publishing, LLC

First Edition, 2020

Published 2023 by Routledge
605 Third Avenue, New York, NY 10017
4 Park Square, Milton Park, Abingdon, Oxon OX14 4RN

*Routledge is an imprint of the Taylor & Francis Group,
an informa business*

Copyright © 2020 by Taylor & Francis Group

All rights reserved. No part of this book may be reprinted or reproduced or utilised in any form or by any electronic, mechanical, or other means, now known or hereafter invented, including photocopying and recording, or in any information storage or retrieval system, without permission in writing from the publishers.

Notice:
Product or corporate names may be trademarks or registered trademarks, and are used only for identification and explanation without intent to infringe.

Library of Congress Cataloging-in-Publication Data
Names: Kerr, Kathleen G., author.
Title: The curricular approach to student affairs : a revolutionary shift
  for learning beyond the classroom / Kathleen G. Kerr, Keith E. Edwards,
    James Tweedy, Hilary L. Lichterman, and Amanda R. Knerr ; foreword by
    Stephen John Quaye.
Description: Sterling, Virginia : Stylus Publishing, 2020. | Includes
  bibliographical references and index.
Identifiers: LCCN 2020025933 | ISBN 9781620369357 (Paperback ; acid-free paper) |
    ISBN 9781620369340 (Hardcover : acid-free paper) |
Subjects: LCSH: Education--Curricula--United States. | Student affairs
  services--United States. | College student development programs.
Classification: LCC LB1570 .K454 2020 | DDC 372.190973--dc23
LC record available at https://lccn.loc.gov/2020025933

ISBN 13: 978-1-62036-935-7 (pbk)
ISBN 13: 978-1-62036-934-0 (hbk)
ISBN 13: 978-1-00-344774-0 (ebk)

DOI: 10.4324/9781003447740

We dedicate this book first and foremost to college students. We hope that the curricular approach, which is a substantive and systemic shift that prioritizes student learning and organizes resources accordingly, honors college students and acknowledges how much they inspire our daily work.

We also dedicate this book to our colleagues; we have and continue to learn with and from you. We dedicate this book to the current, former, and future faculty and participants of the ACPA Institute on the Curricular Approach (formerly Residential Curriculum Institute) as well as our campus colleagues, both professional and student staff. The curricular approach itself, how we think about it, and how we communicate about it has continued to evolve, thanks to all of you.

CONTENTS

	FOREWORD *Stephen John Quaye*	ix
	PREFACE	xiii
1	WHY A CURRICULAR APPROACH IN STUDENT AFFAIRS?	1
2	WHAT IS A CURRICULAR APPROACH IN STUDENT AFFAIRS?	19
3	HOW TO IDENTIFY LEARNING AIMS	39
4	HOW TO DESIGN, IMPLEMENT, AND ASSESS A CURRICULAR APPROACH	55
5	FACILITATING STUDENT LEARNING BEYOND THE CLASSROOM	73
6	LEADERSHIP FOR A CURRICULAR APPROACH	96
	APPENDIX A Ten Essential Elements for a Curricular Approach	115
	APPENDIX B Traditional Approaches Versus Curricular Approach to Learning Beyond the Classroom	116
	APPENDIX C Development and Refinement of Educational Aims Leading to the Development of Educational Plans	117
	APPENDIX D Sample List of Artifacts	118
	APPENDIX E Examples of Learning Aims	119
	APPENDIX F Checklist for Assembling an Educational Plan	123

APPENDIX G
Sample Developmental Sequencing Chart — 124

APPENDIX H
Example of Mapping Learning Initiatives Across Departments — 125

APPENDIX I
Facilitation Guide Template — 126

APPENDIX J
Metacognition — 127

APPENDIX K
Some Potential Pedagogical Strategies — 128

APPENDIX L
The Divisional Barometer for the Curricular Approach in Student Affairs — 129

APPENDIX M
Recommended Resources — 132

REFERENCES — 135

ABOUT THE AUTHORS — 143

INDEX — 147

FOREWORD

Kerr, Edwards, Tweedy, Lichterman, and Knerr have authored a book that powerfully illustrates the benefits of adopting a curricular approach for fostering student learning beyond the classroom. The explicit use of *curricular* helps readers understand that the approach is purposeful, structured, and intended to foment learning among students.

When I was an undergraduate student at James Madison University (JMU), my mom passed away during my first year of college in October 1998. As a shy 18-year-old, I was overwhelmed by the largeness of my new campus. I graduated from a private Christian school with 17 other people. Attending a campus with an incoming class of 3,000-plus students was a major transition. Given my introverted nature, I had trouble making friends during my first semester, and my mom's passing impacted me more than I could convey. I desperately needed my resident adviser (RA) to check in on me to ask how I was doing, and yet my RA was largely absent during my first year. I returned to campus following the funeral and did not share this monumental life event with anyone. I kept to myself, not knowing how to make sense of my palpable grief.

I decided to become an RA the following year in order to show up in ways that my RA did not; I wanted to check in on residents, ask how their transition to college was going, and support them in navigating some of the challenges that come with college (e.g., classes, homesickness, getting involved in cocurricular opportunities, making friends, responsible alcohol consumption). During my senior year, I was a hall director of Shorts Hall, one of the substance-free residence halls on campus.

When I reflect on this time, I am both grateful for the opportunity to have such a large responsibility as an undergraduate student and baffled and alarmed that I did not cause more harm, as I had little understanding of what I was doing. Sure, I attended hall director training over the summer and grew immensely during my two previous years as an RA. I developed my own supervisory style, figured out how to give my RAs feedback, and learned how to handle crises ranging from homesickness to alcohol poisoning, to mice in the building, to roommate conflicts. And yet, reflecting back, I often think, "Who the hell thought it was a good idea to give an undergraduate student such a role?!" I was not ready and often made decisions because they felt good, through the process of elimination, or guessing.

I share this story because I would have benefited immensely from a curricular approach during my time as both an RA and a hall director. Rather than simply guessing or relying on my best judgment (nonetheless, an important skill), using a more systematic, scholarship-focused approach would have yielded stronger and more consistent learning and development among RAs and residents.

As the authors write,

> A curricular approach aligns the mission, goals, outcomes, and practices of a student affairs division, department, or other unit that works to educate students beyond the classroom with those of the institution and organizes intentional and developmentally sequenced strategies to facilitate student learning. (p. 12, this volume)

In the following sections, I discuss four issues with which I was grappling as an undergraduate student during my first year of college and as a hall director during my fourth year to illustrate the unique benefits of adopting a curricular approach and why this book is sorely needed and timely.

Processing Grief

Early in my college tenure, I experienced a traumatic event—the passing of my mom. I did not have the tools to navigate this death, while also transitioning to a new setting. JMU had an institutional priority in supporting students' well-being. Had my RA been interested in his role, he might have known this institutional priority and thus been aware of learning aims and outcomes that would guide engagement of residents that involved them being able to establish healthy coping behaviors. Although I did not necessarily use visibly irresponsible coping mechanisms, such as turning to alcohol, the methods of avoiding and internalizing my grief were equally ineffective.

My RA could have been guided to ask each resident to devise two goals for responsible coping mechanisms as they approached conflicts or to identify two campus resources for processing grief. My goal might have been, "I will use a journal to reflect on my thoughts when I feel overwhelmed." Given my introverted nature, writing in this journal may have aided me in making sense of my grief in a way that was comfortable for me. Another student might seek a counselor for addressing a similar challenge.

Transitioning to a New Environment

As seen in my story, I experienced major culture shock as a first-year student: I went from a conservative, sheltered, Christian context where dancing, parties, alcohol, and sex before marriage were frowned upon to a campus where a number of my peers engaged in all these activities. First-year students, in general, experience transition issues in college. An environment that supported students in making at least one connection during the first week of college and that had intentional processes in place to foster these connections would have helped me. I remember my RA holding a floor meeting to tell us the rules of the residence hall, but he provided no structured ways for us to connect with each other.

One potential learning outcome might be, "As a result of attending James Madison University, students will be able to successfully navigate diverse learning environments." The specific strategy-level outcome, then, for my residence hall might be, "As a result of participating in the opening floor meeting, students will identify one person in the hall with whom they can connect." The hope, as students experience transition challenges, is that they have at least one other person with whom to process. RAs can then aid residents in knowing how to engage in these structured conversations, the signs of needing help, and how to ask for help. Readers see how a curricular approach moves this fuzzy broad issue of *transition* to something more specific and tangible.

Engaging in Dialogue With Resident Advisers

At this point, I have pointed out the lack of attention my RA provided. I did not know his reasons for not engaging with me as a resident. Perhaps he was overwhelmed with the RA role or did not have enough structure to understand how to engage residents. Perhaps he was scared of approaching us. Whatever the reason, hall directors can work with RAs to intentionally facilitate learning tied to broader goals and outcomes for their work with residents, with regular ways to assess progress toward these goals. Rather than requiring RAs to simply meet with residents or walk the floor weekly, more thought can go into what happens during these meetings. Helping RAs develop questions to guide interactions can facilitate learning and yield more substantive reflection and gather information from residents. The authors of this book effectively illustrate repeatedly the importance of being intentional in one's approaches as an educator.

Choosing to Live Substance Free

One element I encountered as a hall director was navigating the substance-free living environment. Parents wanted their children to adopt this lifestyle, and some did, while many others refused due to the restriction this lifestyle caused. Yet, I never had intentional conversations with residents about the *why* behind their decisions. The use of a curricular approach would have enabled me to reflect on strategies for engaging residents in these conversations about the *why*.

For example, during the initial floor meeting, I could have supported my RAs in working with their residents to reflect on their reasons for living in Shorts Hall. Following this individual silent reflecting time, RAs could engage residents in thinking through the following learning outcome: "As a result of the opening floor meeting in Shorts Hall, residents will be able to articulate three differences between substance-free living and substance living" and/or "As a result of attending the opening floor meeting, residents will be able to convey three benefits of substance-free living." This goal is tangible and will foster initial dialogues between RAs and residents about what they noted, as well as what differences they see in what they wrote as compared to their peers.

These four issues are examples to underscore the unique benefits of what a curricular approach offers educators. It enables educators to be intentional in fostering student learning, rather than relying on intuition.

The *how* of the book is perhaps the most compelling component. In the third chapter, the authors provide a useful framework for how institutional leaders move from mission statements to learning aims and facilitation guides. This funnel approach to facilitating learning provides a helpful image for educators to use to make sense of the difficult task of fostering student learning. In sum, to move from intuition to structured learning necessitates what the authors claim is a paradigm shift, where one begins to see learning as more systematic with concrete ways to assess that learning. For educators ready to embrace this change, this book is a must-read.

Stephen John Quaye
The Ohio State University
Columbus, Ohio

PREFACE

In 2006, in *About Campus*'s "Beyond Seat Time and Student Satisfaction: A Curricular Approach to Residential Education," two of us (Kerr and Tweedy) reflected on the effectiveness of our traditional residence hall programming at the University of Delaware (UD) and asserted that programming models and wellness wheels lacked educational integrity. Kerr, Tweedy, and other colleagues at UD began seeking a new approach that would offer more intentional and sequenced learning guided by outcomes that could be assessed and improved on over time. Staff members at UD began sharing the initial thinking and application of this approach when they hosted the first American College Personnel Association (ACPA) College Student Educators International Residential Curriculum Institute (RCI) at UD in January 2007.

Kerr and Tweedy invited another one of us (Edwards) to attend this first RCI. He declined these kinds of invitations because he was in the midst of finishing his dissertation and his doctoral program at the University of Maryland, College Park. He has confessed publicly that he was not only busy but also in his peak "smarty-pants mode," at the time thinking he knew much more than he actually did. Eventually Edwards agreed to attend but did so skeptical about both the newness of this approach and its potential effectiveness. Sitting in the audience during a closing session at the conclusion of the institute, Edwards found himself thinking that this approach was both revolutionary and obvious. He found it revolutionary because his whole paradigm for thinking about student affairs work had been completely shifted. Simultaneously, he found it obvious because once his paradigm had been shifted this new approach was not more complicated or difficult. The title of this book emerged from those reflections. The authors hope readers will find this book helpful in making a revolutionary shift in their paradigm of thinking about student affairs by facilitating unlearning in the earlier chapters and making the design and implementation much more obvious in later chapters. Most of the tables and images you will see throughout the book can also be found as appendices. We hope the collection of appendices will serve as an ongoing resource for those working to implement a curricular approach on their campuses.

The institute has continued annually and is now the ACPA Institute on the Curricular Approach (ICA), reflecting the application of this approach, not just in residence halls, but in the overall student experience beyond the classroom. The institute is not a conference but a series of sequenced and intentionally planned sessions designed to model the curricular approach for attendees while teaching them about the core tenets and definitions of a curricular approach; how to design, implement, and assess a curricular approach uniquely designed to fit their students and institutional context; and how to continually build and evolve their curricular approach.

The 10 essential elements were created by a few institute faculty members in 2009 to clearly define the systemic nature of a curricular approach and to articulate what a curricular approach is and what it is not. These essential elements have been presented as part of the opening plenary for the institute by Edwards and Gardner since 2010 and guide the design of the institute sessions. The 10 essential elements have shifted in wording slightly over the years by institute faculty but have remained principally the same in substance. The elements were first formally published beyond the institute, using language applicable to not only residence life but also student divisions of student affairs, by three of us and a colleague (Kerr et al., 2017) who reflected on 10 years of lessons learned through the institute and practice on campus in "Shifting to Curricular Approaches to Learning Beyond the Classroom." In this book, the authors offer an updated "10 Essential Elements" of a curricular approach (Edwards & Gardner, 2019; Kerr et al., 2017). These elements (Table P.1) are an important guiding framework and reflect more than a decade of innovation, trial and error, and scholarly advances from institute faculty.

The institute is planned and organized by selected faculty who since 2007 have been collectively advancing the growth, development, and evolution of the curricular approach for student learning beyond the classroom. Through the collective wisdom of long-standing and ever-expanding faculty (32 faculty in 2019), institute participants' engagement, and innovations occurring on individual campuses, the approach has evolved beyond the residence halls into many other key sectors of the student learning environment at colleges and universities. Thousands of practitioners representing hundreds of colleges and universities from the United States and other countries have attended the institute to learn how to design and implement the curricular approach both in residence halls and for entire divisions of student affairs. In 2019, the institute served over 500 participants, and it continues to have a waiting list each year and is organized by faculty members who continue to expand and refine our collective thinking and application of a curricular approach.

TABLE P.1
10 Essential Elements for a Curricular Approach

ESSENTIAL ELEMENT 1: The curricular approach is directly connected to institution mission, context, and student populations served.
ESSENTIAL ELEMENT 2: The learning aims, including educational priority, learning goals, and learning outcomes are derived from the institutional context.
ESSENTIAL ELEMENT 3: Learning aims and strategies are rooted in scholarship.
ESSENTIAL ELEMENT 4: Learning outcomes drive the development of educational strategies.
ESSENTIAL ELEMENT 5: The curricular approach utilizes a variety of educational strategies to facilitate student learning.
ESSENTIAL ELEMENT 6: Educators who have expertise, in terms of both content and pedagogy, are utilized to design and implement the desired learning.
ESSENTIAL ELEMENT 7: The curricular approach developmentally sequences learning.
ESSENTIAL ELEMENT 8: Campus and community partners are identified and integrated into plans.
ESSENTIAL ELEMENT 9: A curricular approach is developed through a review process.
ESSENTIAL ELEMENT 10: A curricular approach includes a cycle of assessment to improve student learning.

The curricular approach has been mentioned and recommended in scholarship beyond the institute as well. In 2013, Kennedy suggested that the residential curriculum approach is an emerging model in the field of student affairs. Blimling (2015) synthesized curriculum concepts for residence hall learning in a book chapter, Lichterman's (2016) dissertation focused on organizational changes within a residence life department adopting a curricular approach, and Sanders (2018) looked at the influence of a residential curriculum on the learning of first-year students.

The authors of this book have regularly served as faculty for the institute and have each cochaired different iterations of the annual institute. The authors have all also worked on their own campuses to design, implement, and assess the curricular approach to foster student learning aligned with their own institutional mission and context. Each of the authors has also consulted with a variety of campuses to assist them in designing, implementing, and assessing their own curricular approach. Finally, each of the authors has learned with and from the institute faculty over the years, our campus colleagues, and those we have had the opportunity to assist as consultants. The authors of this book have benefited from insights, challenges, and inspiration from many colleagues along our journey. We are grateful for this collective wisdom and have tried our best to recognize those individuals and contributors throughout this book.

I

WHY A CURRICULAR APPROACH IN STUDENT AFFAIRS?

In the current context of higher education in the United States, colleges and universities are inundated with calls for greater accountability, cost reductions, increased return on investment, data-proving impact, and more. It seems students, families, community members, employers, and legislators are all asking for institutions of higher education to do more with less. Student affairs educators have an obligation to each of these constituencies and to their institutions to make the most of the entire college experience for students, including opportunities for learning beyond the classroom. As families consider cost, location, reputation, rankings, academic majors, amenities, financial aid packages, support services, and convenience (Wyllie, 2018), it is imperative that the student affairs profession consider how the student experience beyond the classroom contributes to student learning in areas such as professional skill development, multicultural competencies, values clarification, and psychosocial development.

One of the authors (Kerr) believes so strongly in the educational potential of learning opportunities beyond the classroom that despite living less than five miles from the campus where she works and all four of her daughters have attended or are attending, she agreed with her children that they should live on campus because of the educational value of this experience. Many families, given understandably difficult decisions about college costs, may not be as attuned to the value of experiences for students beyond the classroom and may make different decisions. Yet, decades of research shows that the entire student experience, including what occurs beyond the classroom, contributes to student success and offers valuable learning opportunities (Mayhew et al., 2016). The authors believe that student affairs educators have a responsibility to do a better job illustrating their educational value in higher education.

Student affairs educators can improve their contributions to students and institutions of higher education by creating mechanisms to better understand the educational contributions of divisions of student affairs and best capture the learning that results from the beyond the classroom experiences implemented as a part of the overall educational enterprise. *A curricular approach is a systemic way to be more purposeful and strategic about how educators who work with students beyond the classroom can best facilitate student learning as an outcome of the student experience.* In this book, the authors offer guidance to help student affairs educators maximize and demonstrate the educational value of college experiences that are not on a professor's syllabus but are crucial to a student's holistic growth, development, and learning.

The need to demonstrate the educational value of learning that occurs beyond the classroom has become more important as challenges institutions face increase, making resource allocation decisions even more difficult. Campuses are more complex than they were 10 years ago, with greater student diversity, increases in mental health needs, evolving alcohol and substance abuse issues, increasing reports of sexual misconduct, and many other issues. Simultaneously, state and federal funding to higher education has decreased while administrators strive to keep the overall cost of attendance in check (*The Chronicle of Higher Education*, 2018). Initiatives such as espoused competency-based education, performance-based funding metrics, cocurricular transcripts, massive open online courses (MOOCs), and employability outcomes are reflective of these ongoing changes in higher education. Rising costs, student loan debt crises, and limited employment options are only a few indicators that the value of higher education is under scrutiny from students, their supporters and families, employers, and legislators. Societal expectations of a college education have also changed. Accreditation agencies want to know about student learning goals and assessment data of gains that occur both inside and beyond the classroom (Fallucca, 2018). Lawmakers at the federal and state levels, students, families, and senior administrators want a clearer sense of how resource investments contribute to student success in areas such as grades, time to degree completion, retention, and postcollege employment (Berrett, 2016).

While some campuses may be investing in amenities to attract students to their campuses, the authors of this book suggest this should always be secondary to investing in the spaces, staff, and resources we know support learning, health, wellness, development, and ultimately student success. Institution leaders' decisions should be informed by what will best serve the educational needs of students, when designing a new building, developing a new initiative, reorganizing a unit, or hiring or eliminating staff positions. The central question remains, how do student affairs leaders make the best decisions about where to invest the limited resources they have?

In this book, the authors describe how to develop and utilize an intentional and systemic approach to learning beyond the classroom, which we have come to call the "curricular approach." We use the term *curricular* not to co-opt the term from higher education faculty, but to follow their intended, if not always fully realized, model for identifying learning and aligning courses and coursework with those outcomes in a sequenced and interconnected manner. We also use this term because we have learned much from K–12 educators and teacher preparation scholarship. We understand that careful and specific design can provide continuity for learners with different teachers. As Parker Palmer (1998) stated, "I have learned much from my K–12 colleagues, including these two things: teachers at all levels of education have more in common than we think, and we should not be so glib about which level we call 'higher'" (p. 6).

The curricular approach is different from a traditional student affairs educational approach, which often focuses on singular, standalone, group-based programs and services frequently developed and facilitated by student leaders. The curricular approach allows student affairs educators to identify learning priorities for students in their institutional context and then make decisions about initiatives, experiences, resources, and outcomes to align with those learning priorities. Table 1.1 is an updated (Kerr et al., 2017) summary of the distinctions between traditional educational approaches and the curricular approach.

The authors of this book have more than a decade of experience implementing curricular approaches on multiple campuses; contributing to the scholarship on the curricular approach; and helping many campuses design, implement, and assess a curricular approach to student learning. The curricular approach is deeply rooted in scholarship about the purpose of student affairs work (ACPA, 1996; R.D. Brown, 1972; Keeling, 2004), student development (Evans et al., 2010; Jones & Abes, 2013), neuroscience of learning (Bresciani Ludvik, 2016; P.C. Brown et al., 2014), critical pedagogy (Freire, 1972/2000; hooks, 1994), and organizational effectiveness (Collins, 2011; Harper & Quaye, 2009b; Senge, 2006).

Moreover, as mentioned previously, the curricular approach is grounded in the scholarship of the student affairs profession and beyond. In many ways a curricular approach applies what scholarship, such as the Student Learning Imperative (ACPA, 1996), Learning Reconsidered (Keeling, 2004), Learning Partnerships (Baxter Magolda & King, 2004), and others (Kuh et al., 2010; Whitt, 2006), has called for systematically, rather than by individual

TABLE 1.1
Traditional Approaches Versus Curricular Approach to Learning Beyond the Classroom

Traditional	Curricular
Identifies list of general topics or categories to which students could be exposed	Clearly defined and more narrowly focused learning aims are tied to institutional mission
Often based on reaction to recent needs displayed by students	Based on scholarly literature, national trends, campus data, and assessment of student educational needs
Student leaders or student staff determine the content within the categories and the pedagogy	Clearly defined learning goals and delivery strategies are written by those with educational expertise
Determining effective pedagogy is often the responsibility of student leaders or student staff members	Lesson plans or facilitation guides developed by educators with necessary expertise provide structure to guide facilitation of educational strategies
Focuses on who will show up to publicized programs	Utilizes a variety of strategies to reach each student
Evaluated based on how many students attend	Assesses student learning outcomes and effectiveness of delivery strategies
Sessions stand alone, disconnected from what has come before or what will come after, and vary by each student leader or staff member	Content and pedagogy are developmentally sequenced to best serve learners
Often in competition with other campus units for students' time and attention	Campus and community partners are integrated into the strategies; content and pedagogy are subject to review (internal and external)

practitioners, or in an isolated initiative. Although movements toward student learning outcomes (Shireman, 2016) and assessment (Lederman, 2019) have had their critiques, the substance of these critiques has been that learning outcomes and assessment have not been done in a meaningful way and have been a superficial exercise to placate accreditation teams. The curricular approach is a substantive use of learning outcomes and assessment to align resources and actions with institutional and student aspirations.

The authors have found and heard from many others that this shift in approach can be simultaneously revolutionary and obvious. For many who have been socialized in a more traditional educational approach to student affairs work, including all the authors of this book, the curricular approach may feel revolutionary as it can turn our paradigm for student affairs work upside down. Shifting paradigms and unlearning can be challenging. However, once student affairs educators have made the paradigm shift, implementing a curricular approach can also feel obvious because a curricular approach is clear, aligned, and intentional and can simplify initiatives.

Evolution of Student Affairs

The curricular approach depicts how the student affairs profession has evolved and continues to evolve. In describing the earliest student affairs practitioners, Hevel (2016) states, "These positions originated as college presidents and faculty members became less interested in monitoring students at the same time that coeducation spread, generating public concern that such monitoring was never more important" (p. 847). Initially, student affairs professionals were support staff providing services to students (American Council on Education, 1937). Expansive research on the development of students morally, psychosocially, and in other ways led to our commitment to becoming student development experts (R.D. Brown, 1972). This student development approach itself has advanced with a better awareness of identity development and the importance of intersectionality (Abes, 2016; Patton et al., 2016; Renn & Reason, 2013).

The call for making student affairs contributions to learning in higher education in earnest began with the publication by American College Personnel Association (ACPA) of "The Student Learning Imperative" in 1996 and continued with *Learning Reconsidered* (Keeling, 2004) and *Learning Reconsidered 2* (Keeling, 2006). Because of this shift to center student learning, many student affairs professionals now consider themselves student affairs educators (Whitt, 2006). However, actualizing this shift from being student affairs administrators or student affairs professionals to truly being student affairs educators has been more challenging than simply claiming the title.

When those who work with students beyond the classroom are asked, "Are you an educator?" most will give a confident and enthusiastic "Yes!" But when asked to consider the question, "What do students learn as a result of your work?" the response is too often hesitant, tepid, or focused on areas such as responsibility, wellness, engagement, career skills, decision-making, or life skills. Ask these educators, "Who do you reach?"; "To what degree do you reach them?"; "Who do you miss?"; and "How do you know?" and the responses too often become even less confident and clear. Like most student affairs educators, the authors of this book have coached, mentored, or helped an individual student or a group of students in an organization or club countless times. Like many student affairs educators, the authors have helped students facing incredibly complicated personal or family situations. But, do student affairs educators have evidence of how they affect student learning for the hundreds or sometimes thousands of students within their scope of responsibility or within their sphere of influence? The absence of an ability to clearly articulate what student affairs professionals teach, demonstrate what students learn as a result, and describe how student affairs fits into the larger aims of student learning within our individual institutions puts student affairs resources and reputations at risk and undermines the educational potential of the college experience for all students.

Each college and university has (or should have) comprehensive data actively tracking the key areas of student success. These key success indicators typically include retention, grades, graduation, and time to graduation. Those who work with students beyond the classroom have very few initiatives that have directly and explicitly been connected to such crucial measurements. Initiatives beyond the classroom with clearly articulated learning outcomes and assessment data are better able to be included in key institutional measures. Recognizing the need for student affairs educators to be able to intentionally and systematically approach their work as other educators do resulted in the creation of the curricular approach.

Critique of the Traditional Educational Approach Beyond the Classroom

Not all the work done beyond the classroom is student learning focused. Blimling (2001) described four communities of practice for student affairs: student learning, student development, student services, and student administration. To be successful, a student affairs practitioner must be committed to all four communities of practice. The scholarship and neuroscience described in *Learning Reconsidered* (Keeling, 2004) argues for the need to think of student learning (academic) and student development (personal growth) as not two but a singular learning experience. The contributors to *Learning Reconsidered* explained how neuroscience has shown us that students do not experience class and out-of-class separately; students experience college.

To claim educator status broadly, beyond the classroom educators should be able to possess a deep, informed, compelling, and collectively shared articulation of what all students under their scope of responsibility should have: the opportunity to learn. An educator also has a specific yet continually evolving philosophy about learning and pedagogies to best facilitate student learning.

Educators are individuals who recognize that learning requires more than serendipity. In the 2001 book *In Defense of American Higher Education*, Kuh wrote a chapter about student learning entitled "College Students Today: Why We Can't Leave Serendipity to Chance," and says, "In order for students to acquire the competencies and skills they need, institutions must intentionally arrange their resources to engage students more fully in the kinds of experiences that produce the greatest gains in these areas" (p. 289). We must also avoid the trap of "magical thinking" (Harper & Quaye, 2009a, p. 7), the belief that simply providing certain experiences or services will be enough to enrich the educational experience.

At the root of many of the struggles with educational efforts beyond the classroom is a lack of a decisive and explicit focus on what students should learn. When developing educational goals for students, a unit will often start with a broad brainstorming activity during which individual staff members' personal and professional passion areas are explored. Some student affairs educators express a deep commitment to social justice topics. Other student affairs educators may express a dedication to student health and safety. Still others may focus on student decision-making in an age of highly involved families. The result is often a stated set of goals for onetime programs, social media campaigns, or special events that may have little to do with the stated educational objectives of the broader institution, faculty government, or accreditation bodies. Much of the work is done in reaction to external events, issues, and traditions rather than being proactively designed in developmentally appropriate ways. The authors encourage student affairs educators and others working with students beyond the classroom to be mindful of where personal passions and reactions to problems from last year may lead them astray and to seek to be more proactive and realize where they can best contribute to the educational goals and aims of the institution.

Student affairs educators do not have to search far and wide for an educational focus. Allen (2006) asserts in *Assessing General Education Programs* that alignment of the campus-wide community is critical in establishing "a cohesive learning environment that supports general education" (p. 91). In a discussion about learning that happens beyond the classroom, Allen (2006) adds that the institution, "as a whole, should support the general education program" (p. 103). M.J. Barr et al. (2014) "recommend that student affairs professionals give serious thought to simply adopting the institutional learning outcomes as their own" (p. 147). Identifying the educational aims should not be focused on individual or departmental passions; rather, the educational aims should be developed from the institutional history, mission, current context, and student populations. Identifying the educational aims for student affairs educators should be a task not of creation but of discernment from the overall institutional mission and context. The educational aims, teaching and learning strategies, and student learning assessment are best furthered by being guided by the preexisting undergraduate education goals of each unique institution of higher education.

As student affairs educators, our measures of impact often lack a connectedness to broader institutional aims or to the metrics of student success. The current dependence on satisfaction and head counts never really tells a story of student learning (Kerr & Tweedy, 2006). Yet, attendance and satisfaction measures continue to be used frequently to describe success or the effectiveness of student affairs contributions to the student experience and to student learning. Asking students whether (or to what degree) they are satisfied with an event may be a good measure if the goal is customer service, but not if the aim is student learning. Attendance numbers are even less helpful as measures of impact. Knowing if 20, 50, or 200 students attended an activity does little to explore the educational impact of the event or determine whether such attendance contributed to (or actively undermined) institutional aims for student learning and development.

Banta et al. (2009) note that satisfaction measures are often an intermediary step taken between counting heads and assessment of student learning. It is easy to measure the number of career workshops, alternative weekend programs, diversity programs, or poster series implemented in a semester, and these can even be used to claim "impact" based on attendance numbers. In a traditional educational approach, this claim is limited because of the absence of clear learning goals, sequenced and layered educational strategies, and success measures focused on student learning attainment. The analogy for this traditional approach is the all-you-can-eat buffet at a favorite restaurant. Student affairs educators offer students many options for experiences beyond the classroom. Some of these are high quality; some are acceptable; and, if educators are being honest, some may be harmful. Then educators leave it to students to make developmentally appropriate decisions about engaging in the learning opportunities that will challenge their worldview in just the right way so that learning occurs but they are not overwhelmed and shut down. If left to make your own choices at the buffet, you may be satisfied, but it is unlikely that a well-balanced, fully nutritious meal will have been consumed. In fact, you may have eaten dessert first.

Hosting a cultural food fest may have enticed attendees to fill the room, but the learning that occurred is questionable and perhaps harmful in how it tokenizes, exoticizes, and reinforces stereotypes and systems of oppression. The essential question for those in student affairs and for others who aspire to be educators is "How do you define success?" If success is measured by attendance or general satisfaction rather than measures of student learning considered credible and connected to institutional aims, then it should be no surprise that the unit or office is given less consideration (e.g., resources, staffing, funds, credit, and respect) than it feels it deserves by institutional leaders. There is no shortage of hard work and dedication in the student affairs profession, but there is a shortage of well-supported ways to articulate how student affairs work contributes to key success factors in higher education.

Pedagogy can also be of concern with traditional educational approaches beyond the classroom. The science of teaching and learning is quite complex and is not commonly addressed in depth as part of student affairs professional education and development. Unfortunately, with the traditional educational approach discussed previously, pedagogical decisions are frequently delegated to those who lack the necessary educational expertise. Complicated content such as ethics, social justice, and well-being are given to new staff, resident assistants, orientation leaders, peer educators, and other volunteer or paid student leaders with the task of designing a workshop, an event, or a dialogue intended to expand student learning. Such a method is deeply unfair to both the designers and the eventual student recipients. For student learning to happen, initiatives should be appropriately layered and sequenced, in terms of both content and pedagogy, rather than the happenstance approach that occurs by excessive delegation. Faculty teaching a chemistry course would never delegate the content and pedagogy of chemistry labs or discussion sections entirely to student teaching assistants. Ideally, faculty members develop the content and sequence of the learning both within and between classes that provide a framework from which the teaching assistants base their classroom discussions and activities. With a curricular approach, student affairs educators situate those who will be facilitating learning strategies with the guidance and direction they need around content and pedagogy so their connections with students is fully realized as an education opportunity.

The reliance on a standalone programmatic or event delivery system is pervasive in our field. Student affairs educators need to expand their toolbox for engaging students in learning opportunities. Student affairs units and others who work with students beyond the classroom should examine every single point of intersection they have with students and reflect on what learning potential exists within that encounter. Do reflection opportunities exist in the roommate questionnaire? With the health center documents? With service encounters? Points of intersection and direct contact with students are more rare than often assumed and should be treated as very special opportunities for developing student knowledge, skills, and competencies valued by the campus community.

It is certainly true that ultimately students spend more time beyond the classroom than within the classroom. McCormick (2011) discusses that "a well-established rule . . . holds that students should devote two hours of study time for every hour of class time." However, McCormick shares that the number reported by students through the National Survey of Student Engagement (NSSE) over a 10-year period when asked about the time they spend "in a typical seven-day week" on a variety of activities, including "preparing for class (studying, reading, writing, doing homework or lab work, analyzing data, rehearsing, and other academic activities)," averages "about one hour for each hour of class." It is estimated that college students have 17.1 hours of discretionary time per week (McCormick, 2011), and there is a great deal of competing interests for that time. Cathy Smalls, under the pseudonym Rebekah Nathan (2006), author of *My Freshman Year: What a Professor Learned by Becoming a Student*, discussed the over-optioned and overwhelmed student with so many choices being presented that many students struggle to develop a cocurricular path. In *The Paradox of Choice: Why More Is Less*, Barry Schwartz (2005) notes,

> As Americans, we assume that more choice means better options and greater satisfaction. But beware of excessive choice: Choice overload can make you question the decisions you make before you even make them, it can set you up for unrealistically high expectations, and it can make you blame yourself for any and all failures. In the long run, this can lead to decision-making paralysis, anxiety, and perpetual stress. And, in a culture that tells us that there is no excuse for falling short of perfection when your options are limitless, too much choice can lead to clinical depression. (back cover)

Each moment with students should be considered a precious moment for student affairs educators to explore what knowledge, skills, or competencies students can develop toward the fulfillment of the institution's educational promises. The competition for student time and energy, especially without a clear sense of the benefits offered in exchange for such expenditures, may be doing harm to students, no matter how great the intentions. For example, a developmentally sequenced, logical, and well-orchestrated plan for sharing directions and resources is important for student learning. A communication plan can help identify if multiple departments are sharing duplicative messages with students, contradictory details, or content that is offered during an unnecessary time frame. The authors have seen this on campuses that align all communication to incoming students through a single orientation office and email address after the admissions process is complete and before students arrive. This can allow for batching information together so that it is timely, included with other similar content, and developed in a visually appealing manner to catch students' attention. A more serious approach to teaching and learning is called for and a much stronger value proposition about the learning potential beyond the classroom is necessary. It is essential that student affairs educators move from basic exposure platforms toward an examination of how each student under their scope of responsibility can best learn in ways that are consistent with the educational mission of the institution.

Rationale for a Paradigm Shift

The importance of honoring students as learners and shifting from teacher-centric paradigms to learner-focused ones within the scope of higher education has been documented in various forms of scholarship. R.B. Barr and Tagg (1995), in "From Teaching to Learning," asserted students and institutions should cocreate learning experiences. Further, they claimed, with a learning paradigm, "a college's purpose is not to transfer knowledge but to create environments and experiences that bring students to discover and construct knowledge for themselves, to make students members of communities of learners that make discoveries and solve problems" (p. 15). R.B. Barr and Tagg concluded that a learning paradigm better situates practice that will contribute to the institution's objectives, including but not limited to retention, increased graduation rates, and student preparedness for postcollege life.

Guiding learning by articulated outcomes for learners has long guided good educational practice in the K–12 context and has now begun to guide quality academic programs in higher education through expectations of accreditation agencies and to permeate student affairs literature (Bresciani et al., 2009). The Association of American Colleges & Universities (AAC&U, 2008) has put forth a set of "Essential Learning Outcomes" that are espoused to be the core of a liberal undergraduate education. Examples of AAC&U outcomes for today's learners include domains such as intellectual and practical skills (e.g., critical and creative thinking, teamwork and problem-solving) and personal and social responsibility (e.g., civic knowledge and engagement, both local and global; intercultural knowledge and competence; and foundations and skills for lifelong learning).

In *Learning Reconsidered* (Keeling, 2004), scholars describe learning as "a comprehensive, holistic, transformative activity that integrates academic learning and student development, processes that have often been considered separate, and even independent, of each other" (p. 4). Authors of that document acknowledge much of the literature that influenced higher education and student affairs to that point. Perhaps one of the most salient messages of *Learning Reconsidered* is the emphasis on transformative learning and placing students at the center of experiences versus simply conducting transactions with students. The authors underscore that students do not have a bifurcated experience of college with student learning occurring in classrooms and student development beyond classrooms. However, campus buildings, organizational structures, staffing patterns, budgets, and other systems are set up in a bifurcated manner that does not reflect how students experience college. *Learning Reconsidered* offers the following seven broad, desired learning outcomes for transformative education: cognitive complexity; knowledge acquisition, integration, and application; humanitarianism; civic engagement; interpersonal and intrapersonal competence; practical competence; and persistence and academic achievement (Keeling, 2004). Other learning outcome frameworks include the Council for the Advancement of Standards in Higher Education (CAS) and the Degree Qualifications Profile (DQP).

In 2006, Whitt published "Are All of Your Educators Educating?" In the article she challenged everyone working with students beyond the classroom to "focus on student learning. Period." (p. 3). The remainder of the article suggested the following ways to do that: Create key partnerships, hold students to high expectations, develop early warning systems, teach students how to succeed, celebrate diversity, invest in programs and people who contribute to student learning, use data-driven decision-making, create spaces for learning, and make all halls learning communities.

A curricular approach aligns the mission, goals, outcomes, and practices of a student affairs division, department, or other unit that works to educate students beyond the classroom with those of the institution and organizes intentional and developmentally sequenced strategies to facilitate student learning (Edwards & Gardner, 2019; Kennedy, 2013; Kerr et al., 2017; Kerr & Tweedy, 2006; Shushok et al., 2013). Changing organizations to focus more clearly on student learning in a demonstrable manner takes more than language changes. Substantive change throughout the organization's staffing, practices, and processes needs to be broadly considered for such a movement to achieve desired outcomes and be sustained long term.

The shift to a curricular approach to learning beyond the classroom moves student affairs educators from being transactional to transformational. It allows educators to honor, synthesize, integrate, assess, and continually design pedagogy in the cocurricular arena. As discussed earlier in this chapter, Table 1.1 summarizes the distinctions between traditional educational approaches and the curricular approach. This series of changes reflects the shift to a new approach to educating beyond the classroom, which educators can adopt to refocus commitment, time, energy, and resources to foster student learning.

The Curricular Approach

Adopting the mind-set of educator over administrator and focusing not on the teacher but on the learner requires today's educators beyond the classroom to understand the magnitude of a paradigm shift from traditional educational approaches to a curricular approach. The foundational questions that are inherent to the curricular approach are "What do we want students to learn?" and "How do we help facilitate experiences that will foster that learning?" Each student affairs educator has a role in facilitating and enhancing student learning (Whitt, 2006). Most experiences central to students' lives at college are relevant: living in a residence hall community, serving as an orientation leader or in another peer leader role, participating in a student organization, attending a conduct meeting, visiting the counseling center, and more. In a traditional approach, student affairs educators often observe existing experiences and associate assumed learning to them. The assumptions may be accurate, or wildly inaccurate.

With a curricular approach, student affairs educators start with the end in mind: To accomplish the desired, predetermined educational aims that have been developed based on research, literature, data, and institution specifics, how can these student experiences be tailored, modified, or changed based on good pedagogy to facilitate learning? These ends, or learning aims, are grounded in the institutional context and as such are unique to meet the institutional mission and purpose as well as the student background, needs, and experiences. Achieving the learning aims may mean providing information on conflict resolution, offering activities to practice applying conflict resolution strategies, and carefully crafting opportunities for students to reflect and engage in their own learner-directed meaning-making. If initiatives do not serve an educational purpose, why are resources being invested in them, instead of something that does have educational merit? Students' diverse approaches to learning are incorporated, and assessment, both qualitative and quantitative, is used to foster a cycle of continuous improvement to enhance student learning and improve the effectiveness of educational strategies.

In addition to the distinction of applying scholarship, and use of learning outcomes and pedagogy, the curricular approach represents optimal stewardship of resources. The art of maximizing resources is most evident when an entire division implements the approach to achieve shared learning goals. With previous approaches, student affairs staff members' efforts were typically not coordinated; thus, duplication, redundancy, and competition within and among units often occurred. Staff members attempting to devise deliverable content in isolation of division colleagues often struggled. There may have been experts within another department at the institution who could have provided content better or may have been better positioned to reach learners.

By planning educational strategies in a developmentally sequenced manner, student affairs educators and others have the capacity to better utilize resources of funding, staff and student time, energy, and focus. Further, student affairs divisions with shared student learning goals can maximize the use of resources by reviewing the nature, timing, and assessment of educational strategies to remove unnecessary redundancy and plan integration and reinforcement that is useful in the student learning process.

While a curricular approach has been utilized in K–12 education and in the academic affairs area of higher education for a long time, it is a novel approach to learning beyond the classroom, applied in practice initially within the housing and residence life functional area and now permeating philosophies and priorities to broader campus contexts. There is nothing about this approach that ties it to housing as a functional area. Since the first Residential Curriculum Institute in 2007, the authors have seen more and more institutions launching a curricular approach as a student affairs division or expanding from a residential curriculum to a divisional curriculum. Coordinated and articulated institutional goals for the student experience beyond the classroom, across a division of student affairs, allow for different departments to organize their educational initiatives and strategies to be in alignment and foster integration of educational initiatives throughout the student experience.

Impact of This Change

Shifting from a traditional approach to educating beyond the classroom to a curricular approach can be a time-consuming and painstaking process; however, when fully actualized the authors have found it incredibly rewarding for students, staff, and the institution. Because each set of learning aims and strategies to achieve these aims is unique to the institution and its students, it is hard to compare the results across institutions. When the goals and outcomes differ as well as the educational strategies and student experiences, apples to apples comparisons are impossible. However, the authors do see trends emerging across institutions from the data schools use to assess their own curricular efforts.

The most important gains the authors have observed on their own campuses and through their work with colleagues throughout the United States and Canada are student learning gains. Student affairs divisions and other units can demonstrate clear student gains connected to institutional goals in specific knowledge, skill, and competency areas. For instance, one department of residence life at a midsized liberal arts institution on the East Coast was highlighted as a model during the presentation by the accreditation team not only for how student affairs staff could use learning outcomes and assessment but also for how academic units could do so.

The ongoing cycle of continuous improvement can be professionally energizing. Staff working with students beyond the classroom have seen fallacies in their initial assumptions and frameworks and made immediate improvements. One of the most common thoughts the authors hear from new professionals specifically after implementing a curricular approach is, "I finally get to use my master's degree." Engaging thoughtfully about student needs, designing content and pedagogy to align, implementing systemically, and utilizing assessment to see where the learning aims are progressing and how improvements can be made is rewarding. With clearly stated student learning goals, students are demonstrating their ability to move from being passive recipients of learning to actors in the dynamic learning process.

The shared student learning–focused language within and between units has also been reported as a strong benefit on campuses the authors have assisted. We have seen shared language reduce silos to foster real collaboration and to make student learning more seamless. Educational strategies are developed and implemented in a proactive manner rather than as a reaction to the latest issue on campus. Competition between (or among) departments is replaced with collaboration, making units and divisions nimbler and more responsive. Instead of being experts on campus for how to order the right number of T-shirts by size or how to throw a social event, student affairs educators are called on for their new and developing expertise on learning outcomes, assessment, and pedagogy. One large institution in the Southeast found it saved 80% of the residence life programming budget in their first year of implementation of their curricular approach. This $80,000 in savings came almost exclusively from not needing to buy pizza to cajole students to attend poorly planned and organized programs. When students can engage in high-quality, well-planned, and meaningful learning experiences, they seek them out. This institution was able to shift those resources to leadership initiatives by developing retreats, inviting speakers, offering self-assessments, and more. Many student affairs educators who have made this shift find themselves engaged in different conversations on campus such as being invited to join the accreditation team, to sit on the advisory board for the center for teaching and learning, or to contribute meaningfully to the faculty senate's development of learning goals and outcomes for general education.

The curricular approach grows campus partnerships that connect student learning efforts between units in a division and between student affairs and academic affairs. A student affairs division with a statement of educational priority focused on civic engagement and citizenship may find an integrated partnership with a school of public policy. A combined effort by the counseling center, student wellness, and student health units may connect with courses in public health policy to further the use of positive social norming as a pedagogy. A student union staff may develop a slate of speakers and entertainers that furthers elements of the campus common read book selected by the faculty that all incoming students read. Many possibilities arise when articulated educational aims are shared among student affairs and other educators and when those educators can connect, align, and integrate student learning strategies. For example, when the strategic enrollment management plan called for an increase in available short courses (eight-week courses starting halfway through the semester) at one of the author's institutions, the dean of University College reached out to Residential Life and requested assistance in designing these courses because of the success with the curriculum Residential Life was offering on that campus. The curricular approach provides many new opportunities for partnership and allows student affairs educators to better demonstrate the value added to the educational experience.

College and university success is measured most commonly by retention and graduation rates and increasingly by success after graduation. While it is difficult to prove causality, increases in persistence and retention to the institution as well as to individual learning experiences such as living on campus have been very common. One large institution in the Midwest saw a 6% increase in first-year to second-year retention during the first three years of the implementation of their curricular approach in the residence halls. Promising measures positively connected to student retention and graduation do exist, such as increases in student sense of belonging, student satisfaction with the overall learning environment, student engagement, and student self-efficacy. Campuses have seen their trends increase in a positive direction on national assessments like Skyfactor Benchmark surveys, NSSE, and first-year experience surveys.

Other indirect but important measures attributed to the curricular approach include deepening connections between students and professional and paraprofessional staff members. Direct engagement in the student learning process has afforded many educators the opportunity to engage with students in a proactive rather than reactive manner. Through a curricular approach, learning goals and points of connection are designed and implemented systematically, not by happenstance. One large public institution in the Northeast saw a 147% increase in their care and concern reports, which allowed them to be aware of more student issues when they were at a lower level and intervention could result in learning and a more positive outcome.

Though not an intended product, many institutions the authors have worked with and attended report as much as a 20–30% reduction in student conduct incident reports and hearings following the implementation of a curricular approach. One large public institution in the Midwest saw a 50% reduction in conduct reports and hearings. Results such as these often come from learning goals and outcomes that emphasize a different way of conceptualizing community and implementation plans that actualize community members holding each other accountable. In residence life and housing, the reduction in serious conduct issues has allowed resident assistants to shift energies toward coaching and advising and away from general authority and security roles. New professional-level staff have expressed time and time again that they have a renewed appreciation for their work when they view it from the role of teaching and learning rather than administrative management with elusive gains from their programming efforts, resulting in increased professional staff engagement and retention (for the right reasons).

Conclusion

Student affairs educators in environments beyond the classroom in higher education have advanced their practice to mirror models most familiar to those within the classroom in higher education and K–12. The priority has been to foster student learning and development toward institutional aims and outcomes. While a wide range of internal and external considerations exists for institutions of higher education, attention to how student affairs practice can evolve to further prioritize student learning and development in all spaces of campus is critical.

In this book, the authors provide context and guidance for understanding and implementing the curricular approach to education beyond the classroom. In chapter 2, we outline what a curricular approach entails, focusing on the "10 Essential Elements." In chapter 3, we discuss how staff in a department or division can identify learning aims for students to guide their curricular approach. In chapter 4, we detail how to tangibly develop components for implementing a curricular approach. Chapter 5 explores how students learn and how we can best facilitate student learning beyond the classroom. In chapter 6, we share insights on leading differently for a curricular approach. The process of designing a full-year or four-year sequenced curriculum for student learning requires division and department leaders to ask themselves hard questions, deeply examine institutional priorities, and develop congruence on not only what students should have the opportunity to learn but also how students best learn beyond the classroom. The simple act of engaging with such questions starts the process for improving student learning and success.

2

WHAT IS A CURRICULAR APPROACH IN STUDENT AFFAIRS?

A curricular approach allows student affairs educators to clarify what students should have the opportunity to learn in their time beyond the classroom and how students can best achieve this learning. The curricular approach to learning beyond the classroom operates in a manner like a curriculum for a major and a syllabus for a class, though the instructional strategies differ substantially. A curriculum is an articulation of broad learning goals refined and further articulated by student learning outcomes and a comprehensive, intentional, and developmentally sequenced student engagement and delivery plan. This plan provides focus, clarity, and a process for continuously improving design and implementation through assessment.

The use of a curricular approach in student affairs is both the mind-set and strategy to contribute to student learning in a manner that makes aspirations, inputs, process, and outputs visible, explicit, and available for improvement. Simply adding learning outcomes to existing approaches of practice misses the point. Rather, a curricular approach systematically transforms the degree of intentionality for designing learning experiences collectively and in a sequenced and integrated way that allows students to maximize their learning in deeper and more meaningful ways and allows student affairs educators to articulate this learning to students, colleagues, accrediting bodies, and budget offices. Most significantly, the approach, when overlaid with an equity and justice lens, allows student affairs educators to attend to the diversity of students on campus. The results of using a curricular approach differentiate it from a more superficial change that is unlikely to improve learning and student success.

A curricular approach begins with a broad aspirational statement of learning for students (similar to a general course catalogue statement of what a student will gain by majoring in a particular discipline), then is further refined through an articulation of key goals for learning (similar to the listing of core competencies for a discipline), which are then translated into the creation of an intentional student experience that leads to learning (the courses, course syllabi, course activities and assignments, and facilitation guides). The curricular approach pushes student affairs educators to be clear about their student learning goals and outcomes so they can provide a network of learning opportunities to attempt to reach each student rather than a select few who attend workshops, events, and leadership opportunities.

Challenging the Status Quo

When two of the authors (Kerr and Tweedy) eliminated the traditional programming and workshop approach as their primary means to reach students and began developing the curricular approach to student learning in residence halls at the University of Delaware (UD), it was not because they were unsuccessful programmers. The department program frequency and attendance statistics were quite strong and impressive. The various workshops and event series were points of pride by the department and the institution. The department was reasonably resourced and hired dedicated and innovative staff. Satisfaction surveys consistently demonstrated highly positive results. However, as professional staff in the department began to think more critically about "success," they were influenced by discussions about *The Student Learning Imperative* (ACPA, 1996). The members of the organization had been making a shift to assess and examine not only what was delivered but also what students gained because of successful delivery approaches. Through years of multipronged assessment, educational initiative approach changes, staff training adjustments, and program frequency changes, the answers to the long-term question "What are students learning in the residence halls?" were far less than satisfactory.

These were tough conversations that helped the UD professional staff members realize that students were not achieving the learning that had been hoped for, assumed, and claimed. They became aware that they were annually pouring resources (human, financial, emotional, and psychological) into things that had little measurable impact. Instead of asking what programs they should offer and how these student programs supported their goals, they started with a single question: What should students learn because of their residence hall experience on our campus?

The UD staff members eventually formulated a step-by-step process to guide their collective understanding of what students should learn in the residence halls based on their institution's mission, other institutional documents or artifacts, and their specific populations of students, and then to organize the teaching, learning, and environmental inputs. This naturally led to the adoption of approaches inspired by academic disciplines and the K–12 arena for organizing broad learning goals and more specific outcomes appropriate for distinctive college learning environments. Just as broad student learning goals are broken down into more specific learning outcomes and then sequenced across and within courses, the authors realized this approach could also be applied to student learning beyond the classroom in higher education.

The UD staff and the authors of this book were certainly not the only ones focused on the question of student learning gains beyond the classroom. CAS (2019) had been exploring ways to improve higher education inside and outside the classroom since 1979. At the time that Kerr, Tweedy, and colleagues were exploring this new way of approaching student affairs work, ACPA's Commission for Housing and Residential Life, with Kerr serving as commission chair, was exploring *Learning Reconsidered* (Keeling, 2004) and its implications for practice. ACPA provided support to UD as it created the Residential Curriculum Institute (RCI), now the ACPA Institute on the Curricular Approach (ICA). The institute began with approximately 50 participants in January 2007 and has expanded to over 400 participants and a waiting list of 100 as of this writing in 2019. Numerous student affairs preparatory programs now focus on the study of student learning and learning outcome assessment for the newest members of the profession. While change is incremental, recent graduates with master's degrees are ever more capable and often better equipped than the more seasoned staff members to address questions about outcomes, assessment, and evidence-based student success frameworks.

As more student affairs professionals were drawn to a curricular approach to learning beyond the classroom, opportunities for innovation, missteps, and scholarly advances while exploring this shift in thinking eventually led to the development of a guiding framework, which is referred to as "The 10 Essential Elements of a Curricular Approach" (Edwards & Gardner, 2019; Kerr et al., 2017). These 10 essential elements, when applied, help student affairs educators implement a curricular approach to learning beyond the classroom that is distinctive to, and consistent with, their own institution's aims and values.

The 10 Essential Elements

The 10 essential elements are intended to help educators beyond the classroom systematically adhere to practices that improve student learning, offer stability and sustainability, and lead to continuous improvement. The authors of this book and many of our institute faculty partners have worked with colleagues at institutions that have not attended to these essential elements and have observed the frustrations and pitfalls. Most common is the tendency to add learning outcome language to existing approaches without changing the premise of the approach or the practice. For instance, one institution adopted a learning outcome approach and simply required student peer educators to list learning outcomes in their program planning worksheets. Another institution adopted most elements yet continued to measure success only by attendance counts and satisfaction surveys.

The 10 essential elements are actualized throughout the curriculum design process, and each is necessary to construct the curricular approach to student learning. They are designed to be interwoven and mutually reinforcing. Although the path to applying the 10 essential elements to practice is not necessarily linear, many who have adopted the curricular approach find that practice builds on itself as the elements are outlined. Table 2.1 lists the 10 essential elements, which will be discussed next.

Essential Element 1: The Curricular Approach Is Directly Connected to Institution Mission, Context, and Student Populations Served

Although institutional missions have much in common, each college and university has a distinctive identity, history, context, and vision for what a degree earner should possess. As student affairs educators move through the curricular design process, the vision of the institution must be unearthed, understood, and attended to in all aspects of the curricular design process. Each institution also seeks, enrolls, retains, and graduates different students. Being aware of trends and the diversity, or lack thereof, of the student population in terms of race, socioeconomic status, ability, sexual orientation, gender identity, political leanings, major choices, regionality, religious affiliation, age, and more can help direct the focus of the learning aims beyond the classroom.

Most student affairs educators enter the profession with personal passions about the undergraduate student experience and with a sense of personal mission. This is admirable and is the genesis for many successes in the student affairs field. Failing to temper these passions or contextualize them in the institutional context contributes to continued silos not

TABLE 2.1
Ten Essential Elements for a Curricular Approach

ESSENTIAL ELEMENT 1: The curricular approach is directly connected to institution mission, context, and student populations served.
ESSENTIAL ELEMENT 2: The learning aims including educational priority, learning goals, and learning outcomes are derived from the institutional context.
ESSENTIAL ELEMENT 3: Learning aims and strategies are rooted in scholarship.
ESSENTIAL ELEMENT 4: Learning outcomes drive the development of educational strategies.
ESSENTIAL ELEMENT 5: The curricular approach utilizes a variety of educational strategies to facilitate student learning.
ESSENTIAL ELEMENT 6: Educators who have expertise, in terms of both content and pedagogy, are utilized to design and implement the desired learning.
ESSENTIAL ELEMENT 7: The curricular approach developmentally sequences learning.
ESSENTIAL ELEMENT 8: Campus and community partners are identified and integrated into plans.
ESSENTIAL ELEMENT 9: A curricular approach is developed through a review process.
ESSENTIAL ELEMENT 10: A curricular approach includes a cycle of assessment to improve student learning.

only between academic affairs and student affairs but also within student affairs units as well. Grounding the learning goals and outcomes in the institution's mission and purpose creates bridges across the institution by prioritizing shared educational aims and fosters greater collaboration toward these shared aims. Focus and congruence with the mission, values, and priorities of the campus helps student affairs educators to truly be student centered and anchor educational efforts beyond the classroom to student populations and institutional values rather than to powerful individual voices or outdated and even harmful traditions. For example, if the campus life office focuses on servant leadership, residence life staff members focus on transformational leadership, and the multicultural center staff members focus on cross-cultural leadership but the institutional mission focuses on ethical leadership, then students are receiving very different messages about what the campus believes to be important about leadership once the students graduate and seek employment. The push of individual and/or departmental interests and passions can easily lead to a fragmented learning experience for students, especially if the campus utilizes the more traditional beyond-the-classroom learning approach of standalone and disconnected events or programs. Determining the learning aims for the curricular approach is not a process of creativity or innovation; it is a process of discernment about what the institution and its student populations have been, are, and will be.

Basing the curriculum on institutional aims does not mean that values of the profession be fully subsumed. Student affairs educators can, however, find many points of intersection between the espoused educational aims of a student credentialed with a degree from a particular campus and the aims for student learning and development espoused by councils and collectives on higher education and the student affairs profession. The academic faculty and student affairs educators can and should have unique and distinctive approaches to student learning within their zones of influence, but each should be striving to achieve the broad institutional aims, often developed through a faculty-shared governance model.

Those seeking to identify the learning aims for their curricular approach will need to become excellent students of their own institution. A deep and comprehensive examination, which has become known as the "archaeological dig," is generally required to begin the process and then distill what is discovered into the more concrete student learning goals and outcomes for the curricular approach. The steps to accomplish this are examined in detail in chapter 3. After developing a solid understanding of the institutional aims for student learning, the student affairs division and affiliated departments must develop a clearly articulated statement of educational priority. This priority statement demonstrates the possibilities, while also demonstrating the boundaries. For example, an educational priority might read like this: "As a result of learning beyond the classroom, students will be engaged global citizens." Some divisions brand that educational priority with a label, a word, or a phrase, such as "global citizenship." The authors of this book have seen campuses articulate their educational priority as leadership in action, advancing the common good, empowered learners, sustainability, or social responsibility.

Less is more in this area, and the educational priority is designed to communicate educational aims clearly for multiple student affairs units, institution administration, students, faculty, and external partners. More suggestions for developing an educational priority are offered in chapter 3. It is important to note that the statement of educational priority articulates what students should learn because of their experience and should not be confused with traditional mission/vision statements, which focus the essential work and the aspirations of the division or unit.

Essential Element 2: *The Learning Aims Including Educational Priority, Learning Goals, and Learning Outcomes Are Derived From the Institutional Context*

Student affairs educators can effectively facilitate student learning only if they can describe what they are asking students to learn in accessible language. Student affairs educators cannot deliver what they cannot express. Far too often, language related to student learning is vague, filled with jargon relevant to a particular field, and is inaccessible to student leaders and student learners. Learning goals, like any kind of goal, must be expressed with clarity and purpose to be attainable.

The statement of *educational priority* is further defined through the development of three to five learning goals, which will eventually drive the creation of more specific student learning outcomes and experiences. Thus, it is crucial that the educational priority be designed in a manner that allows it to serve as both a *guidepost* and an *anchor* for the learning goals and designed learning experiences that follow. The educational priority provides focus, clarity, and a guidepost to setting priorities.

Learning goals begin to offer a strategic and often sequenced structure to the learning toward broad achievement of the educational priority. They may reflect concepts such as self-awareness, communication skills, relationship-building, identity, conflict management, cultural competence, practical competence or life skills, equity and inclusion, well-being, leadership skills, social change, or any other domain in support of the educational priority. Learning goals break down the broader educational priority into three to five more tangible concepts. Just as the learning goals break down the educational priority, the learning outcomes break down the learning goals to provide guidance in developing the educational strategies later in the process. Regular institute faculty member Paul Gordon Brown (2017) has described this as being like a waterfall cascading down and broadening.

While the process of creating an educational priority, learning goals, and learning outcomes is described here in a linear manner, it is often much more dynamic in practice. This process is best considered as an iterative process where the educational priority clarifies the goals and outcomes and vice versa. There are times that the full expression of learning goals reveals that the educational priority lacks coherence and requires modification. At other times, the educational priority may be so aspirational that it requires an unattainable number of learning goals to address it effectively.

A caution is offered here that learning outcomes should be both focused and few. Including everything that is desirable without discrimination of what is essential will lead to staff confusion and will overwhelm the educational strategies and staff. Less is more. Setting priorities is key in a curricular approach and will be discussed further in chapter 6. Designers are discouraged from having more than three to five goals and more than three to five specific outcomes under each goal to guide their overall curriculum. The approach can easily collapse with too many aspirations, resulting in outcome paralysis and confusion about when, how, and with whom to collaborate. Such a collapse will doom the opportunity for integration and collaboration within and across units. The scope may be broad, but educators accomplish less by trying to do too much.

Consider for a moment what it would take for a student affairs division to implement an effort to facilitate student learning on a specific outcome such as "Students will be able to construct two goals for positive (or prosocial) community impact during their first year." Such an outcome would require the concerted efforts of new student orientation, residence life, career services, and the dean of students office. If student affairs educators are to take student learning seriously, they must develop student learning goals and outcomes in a manner that allows them to impact as many students as possible within their scope.

As institutions begin considering learning outcome development, they are encouraged to explore a variety of existing student learning outcome frameworks to see what may provide a strong foundation that anchors learning outcomes in the institution mission, scholarship, national best practices, and employer and career expectations. For example, frameworks such as CAS, AAC&U, and various discipline-specific accreditation bodies such as the Accreditation Board for Engineering and Technology (ABET) have strong learning outcome frameworks that may help anchor a curricular design.

This process of developing the educational priority, learning goals, and learning outcomes can be a lengthy, challenging, complicated, and eventually rewarding process. Many student affairs educators have strongly held views about what students should learn. Many talented teams will argue strenuously about their different personal passions and commitments in higher education. Months of work involving multiple partners and perspectives is not unusual, but it is a crucial stage to move a division and units from program services and delivery to a collective focus on teaching and learning. These disagreements are important in both clarifying the concepts and in creating individual and organizational commitment. It can be helpful to remind team members that this process is not about their personal passions being included but realizing how they can contribute to the overall educational mission of the institution. This process of discernment and articulation will be simpler at institutions with more clear, specific, and widely understood institutional missions and purposes.

Essential Element 3: Learning Aims and Strategies Are Rooted in Scholarship

Decades of research on college students, learning domains, and learning processes inform practice. College student identities, attitudes and beliefs, traits, expectations, and goals are constantly changing (Renn & Reason, 2013; Seemiller & Grace, 2019; Twenge, 2017). Other branches of research have deeply examined optimal conditions and approaches to student learning (Ambrose et al., 2010; Bresciani Ludvik, 2016; Seligman, 2011). There is a wealth of resources to tap into when constructing a curricular approach for maximum educational benefit.

If the learning goals focus on identity development, scholarship in this area will require significant exploration and expert consultation. If learning goals are specified in self-advocacy or self-efficacy, the relevant literature must be mined to identify the right content and develop effective techniques intended to stimulate student learning. This is true for any learning goal selected. Those trained as generalists will need to connect with topic and discipline experts and literature to move beyond surface-level understandings of student learning concepts and practices to achieve the learning. A related benefit of such plunges is that they also have the capacity to build bridges between student and academic affairs educators.

Educators of all kinds find themselves designing student learning experiences from a perspective of how they personally learn best. It is common and natural to see ourselves as a normative or representative example of how others are motivated and how others learn, but it is a tendency that should be removed from the design of educational content and pedagogy. Student affairs educators receive formal training on student development theory, identity development, facilitation skills, and so on. These are all essential and translatable to understanding how students best learn. Many of our K–12 colleagues are well versed in the scholarship and research specific to teaching and learning through teacher preparation programs. The authors have regularly found that those who enter the student affairs profession with teacher preparation training tend to thrive in a curricular approach. Developing a sequence of learning, educational strategies, and measures of student learning requires us to step outside of our personal experiences and into the rich body of research of how students at our colleges and universities best learn.

There is an abundance of literature about not only pedagogy but also essential content on topics such as developing healthy communities (Block, 2008), identity development (Jones & Abes, 2013), and well-being (Rath & Harter, 2010; Seligman, 2011), to name just a few examples. There is also essential information about how to best differentiate learning for different populations of students (international students, first-generation students, second-year students, etc.) (Schreiner et al., 2012).

Student affairs educators must continue to move beyond their personal beliefs and maintain a contemporary knowledge bank on the ever-evolving frameworks about the who, what, and how of college student learning so that they can best support and foster student learning and development (Mayhew et al., 2016).

Essential Element 4: Learning Outcomes Drive the Development of Educational Strategies

As noted earlier, learning goals break down an educational priority into more concrete and specific components. These learning goals are then similarly broken down into student learning outcomes. These goals and outcomes guide the identification of the educational strategies—the pedagogy that can best achieve the student learning outcome.

At this level the learning outcomes articulate how students will demonstrate their learning as a result of the overall experience. For example, "As a result of the student experience at the university, students will be able to articulate the benefits of living in a community." At later stages these learning outcomes will drive more specific strategy-level learning outcomes like, "As a result of participating in the study abroad orientation, students will be able to articulate three cultural differences between their home community and their intended study abroad location." The learning outcomes describe what students will be able to know or do because of the educational experience. They do not describe the process of obtaining the skill, knowledge, or habit of mind.

A properly constructed learning outcome provides guidance on the appropriate level of cognitive complexity for student learning (e.g., articulate, describe, evaluate, or create), which can also provide guidance for sequencing, facilitating the learning, and appropriate assessment strategies (Anderson et al., 1994; Fink, 2013). The level of learning articulated by the learning outcome needs to be congruent with the learning experience. For example, it is unlikely that a student can build a plan for community well-being as a result of attending an orientation on bystander intervention, but it is quite realistic that the student could name three effective bystander strategies. Thus, learning outcomes need to be aspirational, yet realistically achievable within the limited time student affairs educators have with their students. Reviewing common learning taxonomies such as the updated version (Anderson et al., 1994) of Bloom's (1956) taxonomy or the more recent Fink's (2013) taxonomy helps educators appropriately progress the cognitive complexity of the learning tasks.

A well-stated set of learning outcomes forecasts student learning opportunities and offers the designers of the learning a clear road map. A key to a successful curricular approach is letting the aspired learning, articulated by the learning outcomes, guide the decisions about how best to engage the learners. It can be easy for educators to default to familiar strategies, or ones that have fostered their learning, rather than seeking the best strategy to facilitate student learning. For instance, self-awareness learning outcomes may be best facilitated by intentionally structured open-ended individual conversations led by orientation leaders and residence hall student staff. Intergroup dialogue (Schoem & Hurtado, 2001) may be an excellent way to facilitate student learning about identity, communication across difference, and equity, but it is not the best pedagogy for all learning outcomes. Similarly, communicating with new students about consent, Title IX policies, and campus resources related to sexual violence might best be done in a large forum for consistent messaging and emphasis by significant campus officials, with a follow-up handout or small card for students to access later. However, a large forum like this may not be the best pedagogy to explore rape culture, challenge the gender binary, and explore the intersections of other forms of oppression and sexual violence. Too often student affairs educators put serious thought into the learning outcomes for their students and then slip by falling back into the familiar educational strategies they have been using all along or have worked for them personally. In a curricular approach, student affairs educators need to be vigilant about letting the learning that is desired determine the best strategy for facilitating that learning.

Essential Element 5: The Curricular Approach Utilizes a Variety of Educational Strategies to Facilitate Student Learning

Traditional programming approaches might include a workshop on nutrition, a counseling center group on anxiety, a campus involvement fair, a nationally known speaker, or a social justice leadership retreat. In absence of a connection to a larger student learning goal, they may miss their potential for impact. As single, standalone events or experiences, they are much less likely to have that kind of power. Such experiences when connected with multiple other strategies toward a specific educational goal have tremendous power.

Consider the potential of a division or department student learning outcome such as, "Each student will be able to articulate key elements of their own well-being." An adoption of such an outcome by several student affairs units could presumably lead to the design of a reflective wellness inventory by student health as a companion to the required vaccination documentation. New student orientation could design small peer-led team-based learning strategies that introduce the success plan framework and evidence-based key elements to consider. The wellness unit and career services unit could develop workshops during the first week to expose students to successful planning strategies. Academic success tutors could develop a short video on academic success resources to be shared with students via email.

Resident assistants could follow up with an activity asking each student to share their favorite resource during a community meeting. The first-year major campus speaker would be selected based on the ability to inspire students on the value of clear first-year success planning and would be encouraged to use language that aligns with what students have already been exposed to through other strategies. The goal here is that each unit can utilize its expertise to contribute to the broader learning outcomes in ways that meet its individual context. Collaborations between units allow for all dimensions of the broader outcome to be met, and careful planning might allow strategies to be implemented in a sequenced and connected way where learning builds over time rather than in siloed, standalone experiences. This approach allows educators to move from competing for students' time to utilizing each point of intersection, functional area experience, expertise, resources, and ways of engaging students to enhance student learning. Tapping into multiple points of contact will introduce and reinforce the intended learning and allow students to move to more complex learning aims throughout the year.

Student affairs professionals have often thought of their work as event and program planning. With the curricular approach, strategy development takes on new energy in that it goes beyond events and activities to consider other learning opportunities. How might intentionally structured, open-ended individual conversations with students provide powerful learning opportunities for reflection and meaning-making? How might conduct conversations lead to new understandings? How might art gallery displays, room condition reports, club and organization procedures, bulletin boards, or social media activities be carefully designed and integrated learning opportunities for students? When the student sees and hears similar messaging about conflict management in the housing form about roommate preferences in May, in the email from orientation in July, in the message from the dean of students during orientation, from the resident assistant at the first community meeting, in the handout at the student organization fair, and in the ways campus conduct policies and resolutions are described in the student handbook, the message can really start to resonate for the student.

Essential Element 6: Educators Who Have Expertise, in Terms of Both Content and Pedagogy, Are Utilized to Design and Implement the Desired Learning

In our work to educate students beyond the classroom, student-to-staff ratios often make it impossible for more experienced student affairs educators to directly reach all students within their assigned scope. Education is perhaps ideally done one-on-one. However, opportunities to work with students individually are rarer than we would like. Student affairs educators often must rely on economies of scale to reach hundreds or thousands of students, which means turning to new staff members, student leaders, or student staff to reach more students. A director of health services, director of orientation, director of student centers, and so on cannot be a solo educator of all students. Although it may be ideal, institutions of higher education do not have resources to hire the number of full-time staff necessary to be the primary instructor for student learning beyond the classroom. Thus, newer staff members, student peer educators, or peer leaders are often relied on to develop content for student learning and determine how that content should best be facilitated. It is unfair to these individuals, and to the student learners we all aspire to reach, to ask them to make decisions about content and pedagogy that we have not prepared them to make. Doing so has resulted in not only missed learning opportunities but also harm being done, particularly in the realms of identity, diversity, equity, and justice. Student affairs educators may have provided a full day of training on justice and equity to staff or student leaders, but often that is focused on their own learning, not on providing them with the knowledge, training, and self-work to adequately be social justice educators skilled at liberatory pedagogies (Adams et al., 2016).

For example, the authors have seen excited new staff or student leaders attempt to implement high-risk diversity activities into opening community meetings or student organization meetings because they had recently participated in similar events at the end of a staff training. While their intentions were positive, they were not prepared to handle the potential emotional fallout, verbal outbursts, or inappropriate consequences that may result from the activity. These staff members miss that these activities were not facilitated until there was significant trust built within the group, content learning was scaffolded previously, and skilled facilitators were identified who had the competency to facilitate the particular topic and activity and who had a foundational knowledge of student development theory, instructional pedagogy, and student demographics as educational experts in that area. Not all student affairs educators are prepared through their preparation programs and past experiences to design or facilitate all learning (Landreman et al.,

2008). With a curricular approach, educators with the necessary expertise for the desired learning are identified and involved in strategy development. This may be a student affairs educator, a faculty or campus colleague, or a community member with decades of experience.

Student affairs leaders must bring their knowledge and experience of content and pedagogy to best situate new staff members, peer leaders, resident advisors, student ambassadors, orientation leaders, and hourly student staff to foster learning with their students rather than expecting them to serve as educational content experts and designers of what students should learn and how students best learn. For example, an orientation program might organize a large audience session on campus policies and community accountability for incoming students with follow-up processing in small orientation group discussions. In order to support the orientation student leaders facilitating these small group conversations and foster continuity of learning across these small groups, an assistant director of orientation could provide each orientation student leader with a list of guided questions and key points to emphasize. Additionally, a health and wellness program coordinator can work collaboratively with a more experienced staff member to review, edit, and update the workshop facilitation guide that had been used the previous year by the peer educators.

Consider a student teaching assistant in a traditional classroom. They certainly do not select the key chemistry formulas that lead to complex understanding of a chemical reaction. However, they can effectively assist students in understanding the module designed by the faculty member, while improving their own teaching skills. Similarly, student affairs educators with the most knowledge and experience of local and national trends and needs, institutional context, and best pedagogy should be squarely in the design role. Their work empowers other staff members, student employees, and peer mentors with well-designed and deeply informed facilitation guides and invites them to add their own personal style within a credible structure for student learning. This approach does not take away autonomy or creativity; rather, it directs and focuses that autonomy and creativity.

Working in partnership with staff and student leaders can help them foster their own learning about the content, situate them to best foster the learning of the students they will work with directly, and improve the learning approach through a cycle of continuous improvement. Advancing the educational expertise of all educators in a division should be a goal of every leader, and every opportunity should be taken to increase the educational design and delivery competence of all involved in the process of educating students beyond the classroom.

There are legitimate frameworks for times when student affairs educators need to take a backseat and let students lead us, as Baxter Magolda and King (2004) describe in *Learning Partnerships*. Providing room for taking a backseat and letting the students lead can be highly beneficial for students as they explore agency and activism. Where educators should lead and where they should support student learning is a constant pedagogical consideration. However, this is very different from asking student peers to be experts at content and pedagogy when student affairs educators have not prepared them to be either.

Essential Element 7: The Curricular Approach Developmentally Sequences Learning

When we learned to ride a bike, we were generally not placed on top of a hill with a shiny new 18-gear Trek and given a push. We learned the general mechanics of the pedals and handlebars, and of balance. We took short, supported distances and eventually dumped the training wheels or caring hands for independent riding. This simple analogy can be applied to student learning efforts. If an institution's general education purpose espouses a goal of developing citizens who create positive societal change, then a student affairs educator may be best served by examining the key building blocks necessary to achieve this aim. They examine these building blocks with an informed perspective of what skills, knowledge, and habits of mind their students possess as they enter the college environment. Knowing where students enter allows one to understand the best starting point and the sequential steps necessary to attain the broader learning goal. In absence of an educational priority and common learning outcomes, various silos often put dozens of learning opportunities into the student environment with little consideration for timing, sequence, and developmental readiness.

When student learning outcomes are written, educators should do so with a studied awareness of students' general level of development and of their prior learning experiences. Student affairs educators must make some assumptions here, and generalizations will always miss some outliers. However, taking the common student affairs phrase "meet them where they are" involves serious study of students and then constructing learning in a sequenced manner. It is no accident that our faculty colleagues develop courses in a 101, 201, and so on fashion. Student affairs educators can benefit from applying a similar framework.

Student affairs educators do not have to start this inquiry on their own. Scholarship and national centers can inform educators about entering student competencies and attitudes. Reports from the NSSE indicate many factors about first-year and senior-year classes. The Higher Education Research Institute (HERI) gives annual insights about students. Offices of institutional research and admissions possess a wealth of information about students that can serve as appropriate starting points for student learning efforts. More colleges are also capitalizing on "big data" producing analytical and predictive approaches to more fully understand the most effective teaching and learning moments and points of educational opportunity. Educators who work with students beyond the classroom can both learn from and add to key data points.

It is important to note that not all student affairs professionals will have their work guided by the learning goals and outcomes of a curricular approach. For example, individual counseling center appointments should be client centered. However, the workshops on listening and empathy that the counseling center staff offer on campus and for student leadership trainings could be strengthened by connecting to student learning outcomes and integrating with the messaging from other offices.

When educators look at student learning outcomes as an end, they can reverse engineer or use backward design principles in the development of the sequence of learning and determine the key points for the learning experiences. The curricular approach allows educators to chart this sequence and map the experience in a manner that maximizes student learning (Maki, 2004).

Essential Element 8: Campus and Community Partners Are Identified and Integrated Into Plans

When student affairs educators can clearly articulate aspirations for student learning and their role in this process, they find not only greater understanding but also greater opportunity for partnership. Partnership is often an espoused value in student affairs, but key collaborations are far more easily identified when educators can articulate desired learning and identify points of intersection. These shared goals and outcomes help everyone see the common purpose in their work through different educational strategies and ways of engaging students. Shared goals help staff members be more collaborative, and detailed plans help them be more nimble and flexible with campus partners by making it easier to adjust and rearrange.

This can not only foster collaboration across student affairs units but also improve collaboration with faculty and academic initiatives as well as financial aid, admissions, facilities, and other campus partners. As noted earlier, the student learning experience is not bifurcated into either within the classroom or beyond the classroom (Keeling, 2004). Their experience can be made more powerful when educators systematically and strategically resolve to connect the threads of learning. Student affairs educators should not bifurcate the experience when developing student learning approaches and plans. An amazing advantage of working on a college campus is the presence of experts who spend their lives focused on the deep study of particular constructs or theories. Student affairs educators are often proud generalists, but faculty colleagues can serve as amazing guides and consultants to assist those educators with specific student learning content and processes and become faculty allies to the work student affairs is doing in the process.

When partnerships are considered, it is easy to forget the tremendous amount of community partners that can also provide strong learning opportunities and collaborations to achieve learning goals and outcomes. Local school districts provide volunteer opportunities for students to apply and practice skills in leadership, mentorship, communication, conflict resolution, creativity, and many others. Partnering with the city council can provide students with opportunities to work with and solve local problems, create art in public space, or better explore how government structures function to enhance their ability to run student government association meetings. There are endless opportunities for collaboration with community partners in ways that positively impact and advance the community beyond the classroom curricular goals.

Being mindful of how students learn and identifying where we can most effectively add to this learning requires us to partner and look beyond student affairs organizations and scholarship. The goal is not to collaborate so that this unit or that unit gets credit, but to collaborate so that our work best aligns with the student experience. Student affairs educators can more fully achieve their student learning goals by establishing mutually beneficial strategies with partners throughout the entire institution.

Essential Element 9: A Curricular Approach Is Developed Through a Review Process

Just as campus partners should be integrated into the overall curricular approach and educational plans, multiple stakeholders within and beyond the student affairs division should be engaged in the curriculum review process. Despite the best of intentions, professions and professionals can fall into groupthink. It is important that student affairs educators develop steps and systems to challenge themselves to avoid insular environments and insular thinking. None of us as individuals or organizations have all the good ideas. Student affairs educators want to do their best thinking and then get input from others across campus and beyond to improve student learning efforts.

It is not likely that a perfect curriculum for learning beyond the classroom will be developed by a small group of individuals. Nor should such perfection be an aspiration. A curricular approach embraces a cycle of continuous improvement. A review process that challenges frameworks, paradigms, and strategies helps educators see things in new ways that is critical to continuous improvement. As student affairs educators work within teams and departments, they can take their language and terms for granted and neglect to realize that they do not translate to a wider audience. It is important that educational aims and strategies make sense to stakeholders. A review process can help test these out. It is important to expose educators to questions and vulnerabilities prior to implementing teaching and learning strategies with students.

It is common for academic units to consider peer review by a curriculum committee in the faculty senate or to bring in expert perspectives through external reviews. Institutions engage in similar critical reflection through accreditation processes. Student affairs educators also need to consider ways to offer what they have developed for critique and further development from colleagues across campus, from experts in content areas or pedagogical approaches, and from professional standards and expectations such as those offered by CAS.

It is recommended that learning aims and corresponding educational strategies go through a broad review process within the unit and student affairs division, but that the review does not stop there. Some may elect to put their learning goals and strategies under the review of the faculty senate to partner with faculty colleagues and benefit from their feedback, suggestions, and support. Others may recruit a panel of faculty, educational assessment professionals, enrollment management leaders, and so forth as curriculum reviewers and approvers. Others may bring in experts from their functional area from other institutions for an external review. The questions, challenges, suggestions, and assertions put forward by these external groups are incredibly valuable in the design process.

An annual review process presents another advantage by forcing the annual curriculum revisions into a specified timeline. Student affairs work is often reactive in nature, and it is rare to find a quiet time for reflection and planning. The review process forces the units and division to carve out time and meet deadlines for educational design.

Essential Element 10: A Curricular Approach Includes a Cycle of Assessment to Improve Student Learning

Assessment of student learning is key to the success of a curricular approach. The opportunity for error in the crafting of learning goals, sequence of learning, and learning strategies is quite high and to be expected. In fact, a culture of celebration of the discovery of ineffective teaching and learning strategies should be encouraged (Gardner, 2016). Continuing poor practices unaware of their lack of efficacy is a much worse scenario.

While assessment of student learning is listed as the 10th of the 10 essential elements, it needs to be developed at the same time as the articulation of learning outcomes. In fact, a terrific test of the utility of a learning outcome is whether the outcome can be assessed. Just as you cannot deliver what you cannot describe, you cannot improve something you cannot observe.

A robust comprehensive assessment plan of student attainment of learning goals is required for the sustainability and continuous improvement of the curricular plan. It may be helpful to think of the curriculum as a puzzle, with many distinctive and important pieces contributing to the realization of the whole. Student affairs educators cannot analyze each piece simultaneously. They often must look at a single piece for some time or a section to understand the impact of each. They cannot assess every portion every year.

Key educational strategies should be selected annually for focused assessment to examine the plan on both a macro and micro level. Assessment should not be conducted only at the end as summative assessment. Assessment itself can be a part of the learning process through formative assessment. Assessment also allows educators to attend to the differential impact that strategies may have on different student populations. For example, student affairs educators can use assessment data to determine if initiatives designed to promote a sense of belonging are affecting all students the same or differently based on race, ethnicity, LGBTQ identification, and so on. This is an important aspect of a curricular approach that is implemented by those attuned to their specific students and their needs.

Student learning assessment skills can be developed over time. It is important that every student affairs educator engage in continual professional development on educational strategy design and assessment if they are to achieve our aspirations for student learning (Gardner, 2016). Just as it is unacceptable for a student affairs staff member to say that diversity and inclusion is not their focus, we should not let student affairs staff members opt out of the professional competency of assessment. Student affairs leaders need to provide professional development to help those who need to develop competency in this area.

Conclusion

Each of the 10 essential elements is necessary to construct a student learning approach that allows educators to contribute to the educational aims of their institution. These elements, taken together and infused with an equity and justice lens as student affairs educators attend to the diversity of students on campus, differentiate a curricular approach from a more superficial change that is unlikely to improve learning and student success. How these elements guide the development of the components of a beyond-the-classroom curriculum will be detailed in chapters 3 and 4.

3
HOW TO IDENTIFY LEARNING AIMS

Higher education, according to 25 presidents who serve as members of AAC&U's Liberal Education and America's Promise (LEAP) President's Trust, is a public good (Sutton, 2016). While many see its purpose purely for individual career enhancement, the learning that occurs at college serves a much more significant role in our society.

> The good news is that the skills—what many in the academy refer to as learning outcomes—valued by employers and critical for employment are the same as those needed for civic engagement. Critical thinking, problem solving, working in diverse teams, ethical reasoning, communicating—these make both good employees and good citizens. (Sutton, 2016, para 1)

Beyond this general perspective of higher education, each college and university has its own educational focus guided by its origins, history, culture, student populations, and more. Institutional mission statements, strategic plans, and undergraduate general education requirements all describe the learning students should experience and how educators will try to achieve this learning.

The student experience beyond the classroom is primed for powerful student learning opportunities that contribute to the overall institution's educational purpose. Student affairs educators must be clear about the purpose and content of the learning they are contributing such that they can effectively implement and assess educational strategies with and for students that foster this learning. A curricular approach helps student affairs staff actualize the evolution of our work from just indirectly supporting student learning in the classroom to also directly contributing to student learning beyond the classroom (Edwards & Gardner, 2019).

Actualizing the 10 essential elements, a curricular approach is achieved by designing, implementing, and assessing a curriculum that is unique to each institution's culture, educational purpose, and unique student population. In this chapter, the authors explore *how* educators within a student affairs division or a department can identify the learning aims for students at institutions. Initial steps of the curricular approach require the identification of an educational priority, articulation of learning goals and learning outcomes, development of corresponding narratives, and creation of rubrics. The authors will define each of these components, offer examples, and describe activities and prompts that may be used by teams throughout this process.

Archaeological Dig

Learning aims are not created, but rather discovered from the institutional history, culture, formal and informal documents, and other artifacts. Educators who work with a curricular approach have come to describe the process using the metaphor of an "archaeological dig," because the process requires digging deep to uncover artifacts, formal and informal, that articulate the culture and context of the institution. Much like an archaeologist studies artifacts for meaning, student affairs educators seek to explore documents, speeches, Web pages, campus newspapers, and more to discover the unique institutional learning focus. From this archaeological dig comes information that is synthesized and then guides the development of the overall learning aims, which includes a statement of educational priority, learning goals, narratives, learning outcomes, and rubrics. This development and refinement of educational aims is illustrated in the top half of Figure 3.1.

An archaeological dig process can be facilitated over a series of staff meetings or at a staff retreat. The inclusion of constituents from throughout the organization and campus partners helps to build credibility, support, buy-in, and capacity. This process should be a deep exploration and involved, but it is also beneficial to not get lost in the details. Rather, participants work to glean the major commitments of the institution from these artifacts. Some educators who work with a curricular approach have found that utilizing assistance from an outside facilitator can help each member of the organization contribute, while someone else manages the process, focuses on moving the group forward, and asks the tough questions that an insider might be hesitant to ask.

Figure 3.1. Development and refinement of educational aims leading to the development of educational plans.

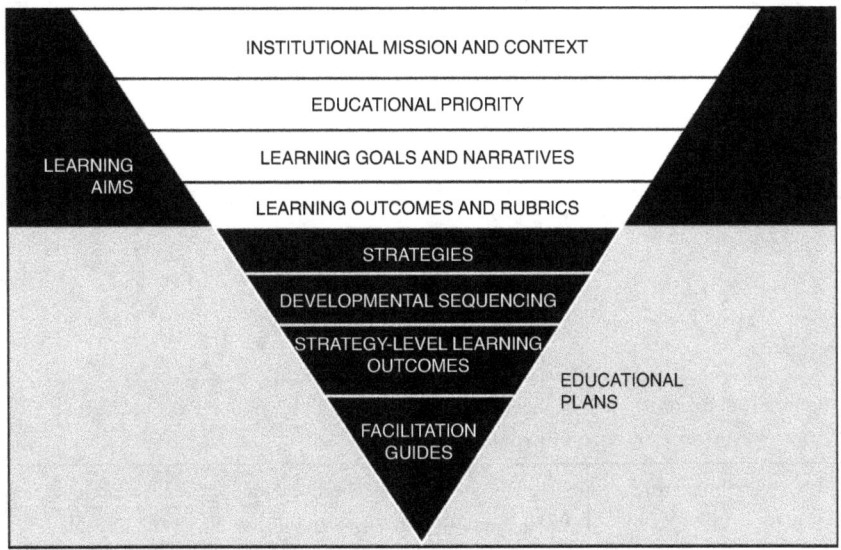

The archeological dig includes exploring institution, organization, student, and professional artifacts. Institution-level artifacts might include mission, purpose, strategic plan, cultural norms, campus traditions, religious affiliation, historical context, campus data sets and student demographics, and repeated comments from institution leaders. Organization-level artifacts could include mission, vision, strategic plan, history, and students served. Student artifacts might include CIRP Freshman Survey or NSSE data, student traditions, recent student concerns, trends in the student population, traditional- or nontraditional-aged students, social group identities, and concerns related to societal and institutional oppression. Professional associations and scholarly literature that serve the organization can include professional association statements; articulated professional competencies; examples of learning outcomes; and scholarly literature related to the institution type, mission, and aspirations. Broader scholarship from the profession can directly link to institutional specifics such as first-generation students and gender expression. All this information is then synthesized to become a statement of educational priority, learning goals, and more specific learning outcomes.

In preparation for the archaeological dig, a core team could pull together key artifacts. Participants may read or scan these ahead of time, but digesting this large amount of information into a student learning focus takes time and discussion. The archaeological dig could include all members of

TABLE 3.1
Sample List of Artifacts

Institutional strategic plans/blueprints	• Mission • Vision • Core functions • Goals • Aspirations
Division strategic plans/blueprints	• Mission • Vision • Core functions • Goals • Aspirations
General education requirements	• Learning objectives • Requirements
Campus climate study results	• Quantitative and qualitative data • Statements on diversity and inclusion
Assessment data	• Division • Student culture
Repository of campus websites	• Institutional leadership: text of speeches and public statements • Signature learning beyond the classroom programs (i.e., integrative learning) • Messaging for campus forums • Organizational charts • Digital publications including campus newspaper

the organization or, depending on size and logistics, a cross-representational group of colleagues at all levels of the organization to ensure that a rich array of perspectives is contributing to the dialogue and vision for student learning. A sample checklist of the artifacts a team might gather to be reviewed as part of an archaeological dig process is shown in Table 3.1.

Several individual and group activities may assist a team in the archaeological dig process. Some prompts to engage participants in reflection in advance and/or at the time of the discussion might include (a) Where does our campus articulate what students will learn by their attendance here?; (b) What are the values of our campus and how do we know?; (c) What are the priorities related to the student experience on our campus?; (d) What do we know about campus climate from formal and informal contexts?; (e) Who are the students on our campus?; and (f) If the learning experience was ideal, what would all students learn?

After individuals or small groups have an opportunity to reflect on these prompts, divide representatives from various offices or departments into small groups charged with the task of reviewing artifacts gathered by the core team. Consider assigning each group types of artifacts to review and critique. For example, one group may be responsible for assessment data; another group focuses on student culture; and another group reviews aspirational documents like institutional mission, vision, or values. Another approach is to have small groups review a large collection of these and gather the major themes. By engaging in this review, participants are engaging in a qualitative analysis, comparing themes across artifacts. By identifying major or common themes and sharing them, participants can begin to see trends and outliers. Identifying gaps in espoused and enacted values can also be useful. It is important to focus on the institutional context and not get caught up in personal passions or what individuals would prefer.

This is an opportunity for the group to be on the leading edge of where the institution may be evolving, but it is not an opportunity to go rogue and move one department or unit in a direction different from the rest of the institution. By using processes such as those featured in this book and an internal or external facilitator, the goal is to foster robust dialogue while reducing the chance for personal preferences in identifying learning aims for students. A simple worksheet, note cards, sticky notes, or a large piece of paper can be used to capture main takeaways such as common language and campus-specific priorities. These note cards or sticky notes are later easily arranged into themes. The key is to filter and synthesize the content into focus.

Technological tools such as Qualtrics or Poll Everywhere may also be useful in this process, especially with larger groups. For example, participants could be sent an online questionnaire prior to in-person workshops. The questionnaire would include open-ended responses on real and perceived institutional priorities, influences, and aspirations for student learning. By seeking this insight anonymously and in advance, participants may be more inclined to devote significant thought as opposed to "in-the-moment" reactions in the face of a confined period in a workshop. In person, a tool such as Poll Everywhere could be used to assess participants' thoughts at various stages during the in-person dialogues and activities.

Another option to involve additional staff would be to create a worksheet to collect input working in small groups or individually. For example, one team might be charged with reviewing the website and blueprint (or other accessible assessment data) and engaging with stakeholders in the office of multicultural affairs. Prompts for the activity might include (a) What key words, phrases, or concepts are most prominent in these materials?; and (b) What are three to five key outcomes students would associate with their student experience? Educators should delve deeply into understanding the institution, scholarship, and more without getting mired by the details. For example, a statistic from a campus climate survey should be considered in the context of other data points. Committing to a grander perspective, after becoming familiar with the details of the landscape, can appropriately inform the statement of educational priority and other learning aims.

Upon completion of the development of key categories, themes, or concepts, it is time to begin using the results of the archaeological dig to develop the learning aims. If a singular major overarching theme emerges, it can be refined to become the statement of educational priority and then later broken down into learning goals. For example, the theme of sense of belonging may be the most salient concept that emerges from the archaeological dig and would therefore be the focus of the educational priority. Similarly, if four major themes clearly come from the dig, those may be refined into learning goals, with an overarching educational priority statement determined later. For example, the concepts of thriving communities, diversity and inclusion, self-awareness, and engaged citizenship might emerge from the archaeological dig. The educational priority might later come together to focus on all four tenets. This can be an iterative process as further discussion, clarification, and refinement occurs. The next step allows for packaging the concepts that have emerged into a structure that serves as a framework for the design, execution, and assessment of a curricular approach.

Educational Priority

The purpose of the statement of educational priority is to connect three to five major themes or concepts into one aspirational statement of what students will have the opportunity to learn as a result of taking advantage of learning opportunities beyond the classroom. The educational priority statement should be bold, yet realistic for the institutional context. It should set a high bar for student learning and inspire staff members, energizing them to do their best work to foster the student learning it identifies. The educational priority should be unique to the institution and organization. The educational priority is not a mission statement in that it is not what the campus, division, or department will do; rather, it is what the students will learn as a result of taking advantage of provided learning opportunities.

The educational priority is a concise statement, typically one to two sentences, that informs students, staff, and other stakeholders what is valued educationally. It articulates the institutional student learning contributions of the student affairs division or department. It does not articulate learning that can be attained through participation in one event, activity, conversation, or reflection; rather, it is learning that will be a culmination of multiple experiences and opportunities.

The educational priority articulates the aspirations of what students will take away as a result of their overall educational experience beyond the classroom. Some examples include the following:

- As a result of the student experience at Example University, students will be able to foster a sense of belonging for themselves and others.
- As a result of learning beyond the classroom, students at Sample College will be engaged global citizens.
- As a result of the college experience at Hypothetical University, students will be leaders for the betterment of all.
- As a result of the student experience at Example University, students will contribute to thriving communities.
- As a result of learning beyond the classroom, students at Sample College will foster more equitable communities for all.
- As a result of the college experience at Hypothetical University, students will be engaged citizens fostering sustainable communities.

The development of the educational priority should not be rushed because it is an ultimate statement of learning for students. It should take time and consist of multiple opportunities for dialogue among colleagues throughout the organization, with input from or followed by vetting by key campus partners.

Learning Goals

Learning goals aid in branching the overarching educational priority into specific learning concepts that are more focused than the larger, broader educational priority. Learning goals are still broad concepts that help provide the initial framework for the details found within an educational plan. Learning goals break down the big idea of the educational priority into more manageable concepts. Examples of learning goals might include identity, relationship, community, equity, well-being, practical competence, inclusion, self-awareness, communication, empowerment, cultural competence, global engagement, and so on.

Learning goals are typically written as, "Each student will . . ." Examples include the following:

- Each student will understand their own sense of self.
- Each student will be able to positively contribute to communities.
- Each student will understand how to foster greater equity and inclusion.

The authors encourage limiting the number of learning goals to three to five. Learning goals help us avoid trying to be all things to all people and focus where educational efforts will be prioritized. The goals are often found in those broader themes that come together as one educational priority.

Developing learning goals is often done in tandem with the creation of the educational priority statement. The themes that emerged from the archaeological dig might be refined into learning goals, or the dig's overall theme might need to be broken down. For example, if the overall theme is global citizenship, the learning goals would be components of global citizenship or what students need to learn to be a global citizen. Different institutions might define and break global citizenship down differently based on the campus context. These broad categories can be summarized by a word or phrase and then further developed into learning goal statements.

Engaging colleagues from all levels of the organization can add significant depth and context to the development of learning goals. Providing opportunities for team members to offer input and feedback for identified goals and then utilizing a smaller group to fine-tune the details before taking them back to the larger group for additional conversation is one way to promote ownership and buy-in and to ensure that multiple voices and perspectives are being considered. Drafting learning goals as a division can be useful to help staff at the department level explore if and how these concepts can be realistically executed within a particular functional area.

Understanding the characteristics of well-written educational priorities and learning goals is critical at this stage of the curricular approach. Most importantly, this content should be linked directly to institutional context. A common pitfall is to compare these components to those on another campus; however, doing so contradicts essential element 1, the archaeological dig, and the opportunity to add value to a given student body. Additionally, these components should be aspirational yet focused on the student population. The various diversities of student populations, or lack thereof, must be considered in identifying the educational aims that may be most relevant to the student experience. Finally, the educational priority and learning goals must be easily understood by a wide range of stakeholders, including students. It is important to use terminology that can be understood, embraced, and articulated by all stakeholders.

Upon identifying the three to five learning goals that are appropriate for the unique context of your organization, the next step is to define the learning goals to ensure that all staff members have a similar understanding. This is completed by writing a narrative for each learning goal.

Narratives for Learning Goals

Learning goals are described by a narrative and then broken down into relevant, measurable learning outcomes. Writing a good narrative in common language, free of jargon, is essential for translating goals into practice without misinterpretation. Narratives provide the learning goal concepts with not only scholarly grounding but also a tangible way to use the scholarship to inform practice. For example, the way in which a campus community defines practical competence may be much different in a highly selective institution compared to a more access-orientated institution. Often, the result is a short three- to five-sentence description of exactly what the organization means by the words in the learning goal. This provides clarity about what successful attainment of the learning goal means in the unique context of that campus community and helps with the development of learning outcomes. Ultimately, a concise, yet descriptive, narrative helps with accountability and shared understandings, particularly given realities of staff turnover.

The following is an example of a learning goal with its narrative:

> **Self-Awareness** (Learning goal label)
> *Students will understand how to be self-aware.* (Learning goal sentence)
> Self-awareness includes one's ability to accurately describe themselves to others in terms of their strengths, values, personality, and social group identities. It also includes an ability to communicate effectively with others (articulating and listening) about a variety of topics. Self-awareness also includes an ability to engage in conflicts in ways that foster understanding, growth, problem-solving, and mutual respect. Finally, self-awareness is not a status that is achieved but an ongoing process of critical self-reflection. (Narrative)

There are several strategies that may be employed to help groups move through the process of writing narratives for their learning goals. Often the conversation through the archaeological dig and following refinement that led to the learning goal includes perspectives that can be used to write a narrative. However, wordsmithing a narrative with a large-group is not a very helpful or enjoyable process. Initially, it may be helpful for a small group of staff members who participated in the large-group discussion to explore the scholarly literature and draft a narrative statement. Having three to five individuals collaborate on drafting a statement can be helpful to narrow concepts. A team might have the same small group develop draft narratives for all the goals or have small groups each take on different goals. Bringing the drafts back to the large group for feedback and input before finalizing is critical.

The best-case scenario is that staff can directly apply learning from the archaeological dig and current research and scholarship to the writing of the narratives. Having institutional language embedded in the narratives can help avoid over- or misusing buzzwords and can provide clarity in marketing materials for prospective students and their supporters, staff recruitment materials, and organizational artifacts. Strategic priorities of an institution, such as integrative learning, may likely be written into narratives to reflect consistent expectations about what students can learn beyond the classroom at a specific institution. Going back and reviewing the note cards or sticky notes used in the archaeological dig activity can help to identify key words or terms that may be necessary to provide context in the narrative statements.

Once the narratives are drafted, they should be vetted with stakeholders. This vetting is to ensure that each department can envision their work in the narratives of the learning goals, and to achieve division-wide or department buy-in. Partners outside the division or department should also be given an opportunity to react. Develop a process to gather feedback from the group on content and leave the wordsmithing of the actual narratives to a smaller group that is invested in that work. This is best done as a package with the educational priority and perhaps with the learning outcomes and rubrics that come next in the process.

Learning Outcomes

This curricular component is the juncture at which each broad learning goal is broken down into more concrete and specific components. If the curricular approach is division wide, these outcomes can be for the entire division, or departments may write outcomes derived from the division learning goals. Developing learning outcomes as a broad division can help significantly with strategic alignment and prevent each unit from going in its own direction. However, developing learning outcomes this broadly can also feel limiting to individual units. The pros and cons to either approach should be considered carefully when choosing which path to take.

Division-wide learning outcomes offer the most consistency across the division, and typically around 10 to 20 total outcomes are identified underneath the 3 to 5 learning goals (3 to 5 outcomes for each goal). Each department is expected to contribute to the achievement of these outcomes by identifying strategies that support them. It is very likely that there will be some outcomes that are not relevant for some departments. However, there should be many outcomes that are actionable for each department. The downside to division-wide outcomes could be a perception that the curricular approach is top down and does not allow for enough ownership, and thus lacks buy-in from staff in departments. This can be offset with a robust and inclusive process for developing the educational priority, learning goals, and learning outcomes, but with staff turnover and short memories, staff dynamics need to be attended to regularly to maintain this buy-in. This type of robust engagement and attention to staff dynamics can create a collaborative bottom-up curricular approach.

Allowing departments to develop their own learning outcomes that can be mapped directly to the division-wide learning goals is the other alternative. The benefit to this is high staff involvement and ownership in the process and often increased commitment to the learning outcomes. The risk is that learning outcomes become so decentralized and diffused that staff lose sight of the shared educational priority and learning goals, and silos are pervasive. Rather than the result being cohesive, intentional, and integrated learning opportunities for students, they are disparate and disconnected and often just articulate the outcomes of the work that has already been happening. This can be offset with a strong commitment to the overall educational priority and learning goals and with leadership that is vision focused. Department leaders need to be provided with clear expectations and with opportunities to share their learning outcomes and to identify commonalities, efficiencies, and areas where shared resources result in synergies.

There are many approaches to writing learning outcomes. One approach is utilizing the formula: Students will be able to (SWiBAT) + Bloom's action verb + condition. In this approach, the Bloom action verb comes from Bloom's taxonomy, which is a hierarchical model that classifies educational learning into levels of more complex thinking (Anderson et al., 1994). The condition is the environment in which this will be achieved. Continuing with the example provided earlier, what follows are learning outcome examples for the "self-awareness" learning goal:

Self-Awareness: *Students will understand how to be self-aware.*
Learning outcomes
Each student will be able to:

- Accurately describe themselves to others.
- Describe how to communicate effectively in relationships.
- Engage in conflict in a healthy manner.
- Practice continued self-reflection around their evolving identity.

There are other approaches to writing learning outcomes that may already be in use on a campus and preferred to the one recommended. Recognizing and following a common or preferred method from the campus setting is another way to embody findings from an archaeological dig. During the development and writing of learning outcomes, divisions could select one approach for the writing of learning outcomes so that the format and language is consistent. This allows for better organization and communication of learning outcomes to each other and to students. These learning outcomes are later used to develop much more concrete and specific strategy-level learning outcomes that articulate the learning as a result of a specific educational strategy.

As in the previous steps, there are many advantages to having a large-group conversation about concepts that will become learning outcomes. Engaging multiple voices and perspectives, including students, in this dialogue can help identify how the learning outcomes can be most relevant, best articulated, and ultimately good guidance for the development of specific educational strategies. The large group can work in smaller groups to capture notes, or use a tool like mind mapping, to brainstorm how the learning goals and narratives can be used to decipher specific chunks for learning outcomes. Using Bloom's taxonomy (Anderson et al., 1994) or Fink's (2013) taxonomy can help identify levels for which these chunks of content can be layered to demonstrate cognitive complexity over the course of an academic year or college experience. Articulating increasing cognitive complexity is a way for student affairs educators to verbally and visually depict how learning aims are structured to honor student development over a period of time. These taxonomies can be useful tools to gauge whether learning aims are both realistic and aspirational.

Like the process for drafting narratives, after a first draft of concepts is developed from the larger group, it is beneficial to have a smaller group of individuals work on wordsmithing learning outcomes. The discussion and scholarly grounding of the narratives and learning outcomes can also be an iterative process that helps improve both products. A small team could work on both for each learning goal and offer drafts for the large group for feedback based on the group discussion and the scholarly exploration they conducted. When seeking feedback, referencing or showing the educational priority statement can help serve as a compass or guide on whether the foundational components of the curricular approach are woven together in ways that reflect the findings from the archaeological dig. Staff members with a background in K–12 education or campus experts in a center for teaching excellence or the college of education may be helpful in drafting or improving the structure and wording of the narratives and learning outcomes.

Finally, learning outcomes should be written to be assessable or observable but without inadvertently being limited by assessment. At this level the learning outcomes are a result of the overall student experience and assessment would come from a variety of mixed methods and not a singular assessment strategy. Learning outcomes are critical for articulating intended learning to various stakeholders, including students. Well-written learning outcomes are clear and succinct. Avoiding the word "and" is helpful for focusing the sentiment of each outcome to one core idea. Ultimately, learning outcomes, as part of identifying the intended learning aims, should be aspirational yet realistic. Assessment efforts in a division or department should attempt to be robust in capturing as much as possible about the desired outcomes and the overall student experience. However, the design, execution, and analysis of the data need to be well managed to be useful. Assessment data can fuel knowledge, but it can also become stockpiled and thus overlooked if not approached strategically in a real-life context.

Learning Rubrics

Rubrics begin to help organize the developmental sequencing of learning goals and outcomes. Like a learning taxonomy, such as Bloom's taxonomy (Anderson et al., 1994), a rubric will assist with both the design and assessment of the learning. Rubrics are a tool for identifying and visualizing developmental sequencing that shapes facilitation guide design, which will be discussed in the next chapter. At this stage of the curricular approach, utilizing rubrics can help with understanding learning goal and learning outcome structures. For example, identifying what level sophomore students have reached in the rubrics can be helpful in identifying the learning experiences that can foster their continued learning. A caveat to this example is that referencing class year is not always developmentally appropriate, as adult learners develop in unpredictable ways. Rubrics also provide a framework for assessing student learning collectively rather than by individual student. Rubrics are a table or chart that depict each learning goal broken down into its learning outcomes and describe the observable or measurable ways different levels of each learning outcome can be captured. Terminology and distinctions such as tiers, phases, or stages are typically used. Categories organize what learning would look like as no ability, then some, then more, and then the level whereby the learning is fulfilled. A "none" category can be helpful, even if it is only theoretical and not reflective of where incoming students may be in their learning. Beyond the "none" category, choose several categories to promote simplicity and thus clarity.

Continuing with the previous example, a sample rubric is in Table 3.2 for the following goal: Self-awareness: *Students will understand how to be self-aware.*

Rubric development can be a useful exercise directly after the division or department learning goals have been articulated into learning outcomes. The theoretical framework adopted within the division or department should then influence the content in the tiers, phases, or stages of a rubric.

Smaller groups of individuals can focus on a given learning goal and can use the agreed-on theoretical framework to draft statements for each level of the rubric. Using rich language to describe each stage in the rubric helps increase the chance of interrater reliability. The ability to come together to discuss concepts can help staff at various levels of the organization have a voice in designing this tool that will be used for other curricular components. The ability for a shared understanding of the rubric can be beneficial, particularly over time with staff transition. Appendix E contains a complete example of learning aims from the educational priority statement to the rubric.

A peer review across the small groups can afford multiple perspectives on the wording with the tiers and can help informally calibrate the content across the rubric by checking for integration of the theoretical framework and reducing duplication across learning outcomes. Allowing individuals across the division to assess students utilizing the newly developed rubrics can help to assess interrater reliability, areas where more descriptors need to be included, and areas where the developers may have missed the developmental readiness of students. Be aware of mapping out realistic but aspirational learning for students in your rubrics, which would shift if you are outlining learning for a single academic year or a full college experience.

Conclusion

This chapter described some key components of a curricular approach that help clarify the student learning the organization is seeking to foster.

TABLE 3.2
Sample Rubric for Learning Goal

Learning outcome (LO)	None	Beginner	Intermediate	Advanced
LO 1 Accurately describe themselves to others	Cannot accurately describe themselves to others	Can accurately describe some aspects of themselves to others	Can accurately describe themselves in most ways to others	Can accurately describe themselves to others including on how they are changing
LO 2 Describe how to communicate effectively in relationships	Cannot communicate effectively in relationships	Can communicate their needs, emotions, and perspectives of others	Can listen empathically to the needs, emotions, and perspectives of others	Can continue to communicate and make adjustments in relationships based on communication
LO 3 Engage in conflict in a healthy manner	Cannot engage in conflict	Can describe ways to engage in conflict in a healthy manner	Can practice engaging in conflict in a healthy manner in some situations	Can engage in conflict in a healthy manner in most situations
LO 4 Practice continued self-reflection around their evolving identity	Cannot describe themselves to others	Can accurately describe themselves to others	Can describe how they have changed and anticipate ways they may change in the future	Can regularly engage in critical self-reflection as part of healthy growth and development

Following are some points to consider at this stage of identifying learning aims for students on your campus:

- The 10 essential elements of the curricular approach, described in chapter 2, undergird each tangible component of a curricular approach. There is no one-size-fits-all way to actualize the pieces of the approach, but brief definitions for components and suggestions for how to develop each component were offered to maintain the integrity of a curricular approach regardless of campus size, type, or other differences.
- The construction of the foundational components should invite participation from throughout and beyond the organization, whether that is for a department or a division of student affairs. Engaging in large-group dialogue is essential for identifying and understanding campus specifics. Institutions of higher education are complex, and priorities are ever-evolving based on student demographics, cultural context, campus climate, and other considerations. Providing structure for each department to contribute to the larger learning aims of a division is important to maintain a coordinated approach to student learning beyond the classroom. Further, garnering input from various stakeholders, including students, is important for efficacy and buy-in to the curricular approach in the short and long term.
- The process of moving from statement of educational priority, learning goals, narratives, and learning outcomes to rubrics takes time. Opportunities for the division to engage in large-group, small-group, and individual review and reflection is important to the success of the curricular approach. Creating a process that allows time for deep and rich conversation is critical as is moving this process along efficiently and not getting bogged down in the weeds. The process needs to be inclusive and collaborative but not suffer from paralysis by overanalysis.
- Student learning beyond the classroom should reflect aspirational realism. Think boldly about what is possible for students and do not be limited by past practice or tradition. Work to uncover ways in which students can engage in learning that supports their personal and professional aspirations as well as the educational mission of the institution.

4

HOW TO DESIGN, IMPLEMENT, AND ASSESS A CURRICULAR APPROACH

Institutions of higher education are being asked to do more with less (Carlson, 2018). Students, families, employers, communities, and society are all asking for more from the college experience, while state allocations diminish, recognition of higher education as a public good dwindles, and increases in tuition and fees do not come close to matching the increases in expenses for higher education (Carlson, 2018). Student affairs educators are committed and dedicated to students, so they stay late to meet with student organizations, come in early for search committee meetings, check emails around the clock, and spend weekends working to catch up. Although this dedication and commitment is admirable, it will not overcome a 15- to 20-year trend of higher education as an industry being asked to do more with less. It has left many student affairs educators overwhelmed and burned out, with significant numbers leaving the field. As Marshall et al. (2016) shared, "Current fiscal constraints within the field as a whole often result in staff downsizing, dwindling material, capital, human resources, and unfilled positions. During these times, increasing employee loyalty, satisfaction, and job commitment is imperative" (p. 158).

A curricular approach offers student affairs educators a new framework with which to identify learning aims, align actions, and set priorities. In the previous chapter, the authors outlined the components of a curricular approach that identify the learning aims: a statement of educational priority, learning goals, learning outcomes, narratives, and rubrics. These clearly articulated learning aims provide student affairs educators with clarity and direction for a common and shared purpose.

Figure 4.1. Development and refinement of educational aims leading to the development of educational plans.

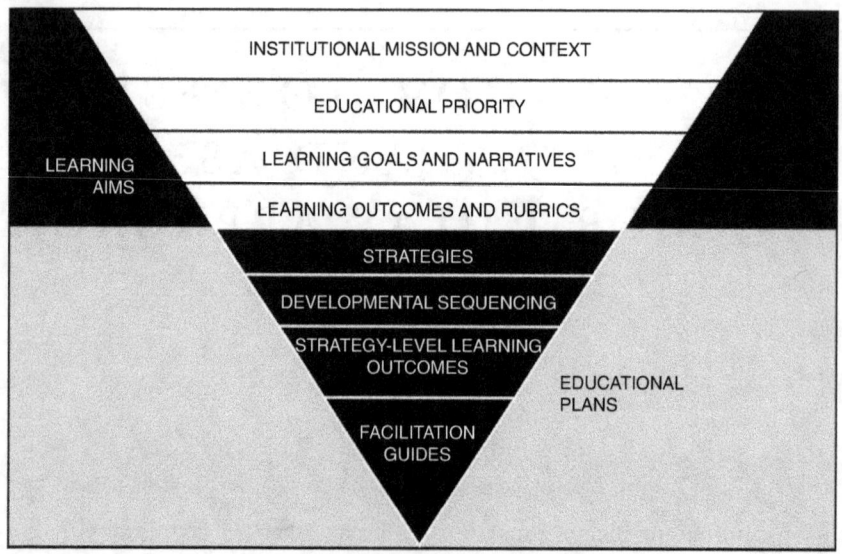

In this chapter the authors discuss educational plans. Educational plans serve to align actions, provide a basis on which to determine priorities, and help student affairs educators create sustainable collaborations across units and functional areas to best foster student learning. The curricular approach at this stage includes developing educational plans that include strategies, developmental sequencing of learning initiatives, and strategy-level learning outcomes that guide the development of facilitation guides (see the lower half of Figure 4.1). Sample activities and prompts to help develop these components are included throughout the chapter.

Educational Plans

While each organization's curriculum has shared learning aims, as discussed in chapter 3, there are likely to be multiple educational plans within a curriculum that articulate implementation strategies across different functional areas. An educational plan serves as a guide for learning facilitated in a particular context, such as the Office of New Student Orientation, first-year residence halls, or the student conduct process. A division will need an educational plan for each functional area, often one per department and perhaps multiple plans within some departments depending on the scope of work in those areas. Offices such as orientation and conduct may be well served with one plan given the narrowly defined focus in those areas and importance of continuity across the delivery of all educational efforts. Some residence life offices might be guided by one plan or multiple plans for different class years or types of residence halls. Educational plans are analogous to a course syllabus and contain in one document the components necessary for successful implementation of the curriculum. In practice, typically it is best to limit the number of educational plans to a manageable number for effective supervision, oversight, assessment, and revision.

For a division-wide curricular approach, department educational plans will contain the division's educational priority, learning goals, and learning outcomes (either division-wide learning outcomes or department learning outcomes, or both). Next, the plan includes the educational strategies that the organization will use to achieve the learning. Then, the learning is developmentally sequenced and individual facilitation guides are developed to structure the learning opportunities for students. Educational plans go by different monikers depending on campus context (e.g., community plans, program plans, educational plans, curriculum plans, or learning plans). Educational plans are important tools to align actions, guide communication strategies, focus staff recruitment efforts and training, and align resources. Each educational plan also includes an assessment plan. See Figure 4.2 for a sample checklist that might be used by a unit within a division to assemble an educational plan.

Finally, documenting aspirations for how student learning will be achieved does not equate to the delivery of actual learning. Educational plans must become integrated into the fabric of the culture and are just as important as tools such as standard operating procedures or budgeting and forecasting of a division or department. Division and department leaders must demonstrate a commitment to empowering student affairs educators within the organization to actualize the learning strategies as outlined in the educational plans.

Educational Strategies

Educational strategies are the ways that student learning is achieved. Each point of intersection with a student on campus could be a potential learning opportunity and can be considered a possible educational strategy. Examples include community meetings, peer education workshops, orientation sessions, conduct hearings, campus events, speakers, video messages, leadership retreats, forms, opening of the halls, service initiatives, digital displays in the health center waiting room, and so on. The list of possible opportunities is endless.

Figure 4.2. Checklist for assembling an educational plan.

UNIT NAME: _____
- **Overview of department** (e.g., conduct, career center, or recreation and wellness center)
  - Mission statement
  - Vision statement
  - Diversity and inclusion statement
  - Core functions
- **Division educational priority**
- **Theoretical framework**
- **Division learning goals**
  - Goal narratives
  - Learning outcomes (for the division and/or department)
- **Rubrics**
- **Overview of learners**
- **Strategy descriptions**
  - A brief paragraph describing how strategies such as workshops, intentional conversations, or retreats will help students achieve the learning goals and outcomes.
- **Sequencing chart**
  - Chart showing how the strategies will be sequenced to achieve learning goals and learning outcomes over time, often by month or week depending on the functional area.
- **Chronological listing of strategies**
  - Content from the sequencing map listed chronologically, often in tables by month. Often includes date/time, strategy, specific focus, and specific learning goals/outcomes.
- **Facilitation guides**
  - Clear descriptions of how the learning will be facilitated for each workshop, campus event, or digital media campaign.
- **Assessment plan**

These strategies must be developed with an awareness of good pedagogy (chapter 5), student development theory, content as outlined in the learning goals and outcomes, and an understanding of the campus context and student population. The derived learning outcomes (chapter 3) drive the identification and selection of the strategies. In a learning-focused approach, primary attention should not be on how educators want to teach this content, but instead on how students will best learn (R.B. Barr & Tagg, 1995).

How students will best learn the articulated outcomes drives the selection of educational strategies. This may seem obvious, but it is easy to fall into the trap of identifying strategies educators have used previously or new strategies they are eager to try and making a strategy fit a learning outcome, rather than letting the outcome determine the best strategy. Guided by the learning goals and learning outcomes, the learning strategies are what educators deem to be *the* best opportunity for students to achieve the learning outcome rather than *a* way to educate students.

Educational strategies best fit the content (learning goals and outcomes), integrate scholarship on learning and pedagogy, and are tailored to engage students in meaningful ways. These strategies are organized around the student experience, not department processes or calendar. Educational strategies should be opportunities that explicitly contribute to student learning rather than complicate or confuse how students learn. Each specific strategy, such as a workshop on communication skills or training on parliamentary procedure for student government, is guided by strategy-level learning outcomes that have been derived from the department- or division-level learning outcomes. Educational strategies should focus on ways to inspire students to actively engage in the process of learning. Educational strategies can be uniquely tailored to address learning goals and learning outcomes while recognizing shifts necessary based on different student populations, physical space limitations, differing experiences and abilities, and other opportunities for differentiation.

One method to generate ideas for learning strategies is to create teams of staff organized to work together to brainstorm potential strategies for each specific learning goal and related learning outcomes. This can be a great opportunity to engage students in the curricular development process as learning partners (Baxter Magolda & King, 2004). Campus partners beyond your functional area can also be helpful in fostering new thinking, innovation, and creativity. To help each team brainstorm strategies, leaders might set an absurd goal for the small team, such as 25 to 30 strategies in 5 minutes. The goal of this brainstorming is to get them to break out of their usual thinking. Then ask each team to work from their brainstormed list to identify the four or five best strategies for their learning outcomes within their functional areas. Here, the "best" could be defined as what could have the highest contribution to student learning within the given context and is appropriate for student affairs educators to deploy without duplicating other work within the academy. Then, have each group report out to the larger group about the top strategies they identified.

Another approach is to ask each group to write their ideas on a large piece of paper. Then, all participants can visit each paper to place a check mark or sticker next to the ideas they believe might be optimal for learners. Often common strategies emerge that have been identified as having significant potential across learning goals, which makes those good strategies to build the curriculum upon. Strive to narrow the list of strategies to a manageable number of four to six core strategies per educational plan. For example, an office of student conduct educational plan might identify core strategies of policy articulation, hearings, sanctions, trainings, and correspondence about policy violations.

In another example, the diversity center might focus on core strategies of intergroup dialogue, cultural celebrations and events, affinity groups, speakers and large campus-wide events, smaller workshops and panels, and bias incident response. Educators may expand this number of core strategies as they progress or add additional strategies that fit a learning outcome, but starting small can help simplify and direct focus when first implementing a curricular approach. Fewer strategies are often better than many strategies if they are better designed, as they can be more effectively facilitated and supervised and reach students more broadly. Finally, working with a manageable number of strategies can allow for more streamlined and useful assessment, which is covered later in this chapter.

Developmentally Sequenced Learning

Developmental sequencing refers to how both the content and pedagogy of learning are organized to foster learning and growth. When the learning is too basic for the learner, the learner disengages and does not need to learn new ways of knowing, being, or doing. When the learning is too advanced, without the right support, the learner is overwhelmed and shuts down. A pedagogical strategy may not be appropriate for the content or the learner. For example, a lecture to 1,000 students during orientation might not be the right pedagogical tool for engaging in conversations across difference, but it might be a good strategy for communicating about the diversity of the campus community and the espoused community values. Varied pedagogies across different mediums at different times in the student experience, all aligned with shared learning goals and outcomes, can foster learning that is retained over time. Good developmental sequencing fosters integration and reinforcement while eliminating redundancy.

Learning is cumulative. Developmental sequencing considers how to integrate what a student experiences around a specific learning goal by intentionally offering them opportunities to engage in strategies and content that are initially basic, then intermediary, and finally more advanced. Depending on the learning and scope of influence, the sequencing may be done over an entire college experience, a class year, a semester, or some other measure of time in the student experience. The sequencing should be developmentally appropriate and consider both content and pedagogy. What students learn during the first few weeks of their first year is very different from what they should have the opportunity to learn during the middle of the year and at the end the first year.

No single educational strategy will reach each student, and, even if it could, no single strategy is the best for each learner. Creating a network or web of diverse learning opportunities helps reach a variety of learners in a variety of different ways. This network might include one-on-one conversations with student leaders and those they serve to help maintain individual rapport and foster reflection; digital platforms to engage students with scenarios and topics that challenge their viewpoints and present new perspectives; community gatherings designed with a specific focus, such as helping students reflect on wellness goals; and social norming campaigns to educate students by normalizing or destigmatizing certain behaviors. This networked approach creates integrated learning opportunities, accounts for various learning styles, and assumes not everyone will engage with each strategy.

For example, a campus might have a learning goal related to sexual violence prevention composed of learning outcomes related to policies and resources, bystander intervention, and taking action. Developmental sequencing would consider the best strategies to achieve the learning outcomes and sequence the content and the pedagogy to align with the student experience. This could mean that in late August or early September students will have the opportunity to learn about consent, policies, and university expectations around sexual misconduct at new student orientation, and that learning will be reinforced during their first residence hall floor meeting later in the week. Later in the fall semester, they would discuss and practice bystander behaviors in their first-year seminar course. In February, at another floor meeting, they might be invited to share examples of bystander intervention they have observed, engaged in, or wish they had engaged in to bring in real-world examples and reinforce the learning from the first semester. During Sexual Violence Prevention month in April they could be encouraged to participate in and view the Clothesline Project, an initiative in which survivors of violence decorate and display T-shirts. Similarly, students could be encouraged to participate in the Take Back the Night march, a protest of sexual violence and an opportunity for survivors to voice their experiences, or students could be invited to sign a pledge to speak out against sexual violence. In this example in Table 4.1, the learning outcomes, strategies, pedagogy, and content are all sequenced over time and the learning that happens within the student experience is interconnected.

TABLE 4.1
Sample Developmental Sequencing Chart

Learning outcome (LO): Sexual violence prevention	August/September	October	February	April
LO 1 Define three actions that are violations of campus sexual misconduct policies.	Orientation: Policies and resources presented and distributed on cards. Floor meeting: Discussion asking for examples of policy violations and resources.			
LO 2 Demonstrate two ways to intervene as a bystander to prevent sexual violence.		First-year seminar: Discuss bystander intervention and name two examples to prevent sexual violence.	Floor meeting; Invite to share two examples of bystander intervention observed or engaged in.	
LO 3 Take action to prevent sexual violence in their community.				Invite to participate in Clothesline Project or Take Back the Night march, or sign the pledge.

Sequencing of the learning in a chart like this can be useful in the design of a plan as well as in the review of the overall curriculum to identify opportunities and gaps. Sequencing learning can help to visually connect each strategy to learning goals and outcomes, reconsider developmental needs, and determine how to better integrate the learning opportunities students may be experiencing at any given time. Having a way to visualize potential learning opportunities and how these intersect with desired outcomes helps improve accuracy and ensures that all parts of the whole are considered. It was also useful for stakeholders (internal and external) to visualize the sequencing in this way to communicate the overall approach and foster better integration and collaboration. For example, articulating the sexual violence prevention sequencing might help align the health center's messaging with the timing of a workshop that athletics is hosting, with the messaging of an expert speaker at the right time, and with partnering with community agencies that support survivors of sexual violence.

During the planning and design process, having a grid that lays out the learning goals on one axis and time on the other is helpful to see sequencing across the student experience and integration within the student experience. Sequencing in this manner is not complicated, but it takes time to consider and reconsider when and how things align. Teams should adjust strategies to align them with other events in students' lives like a study-abroad deadline, finals week and midterms, big sporting event game, and weather considerations. Connecting strategies to learning goals and outcomes and sequencing over time is key to the successful design of a curriculum.

Mapping the strategies used back to the learning goals and outcomes can also help us take stock of initiatives across units and ultimately identify where there are gaps or where efforts are too concentrated. Maki's (2004) article "Map and Inventories: Anchoring Efforts to Track Student Learning" provides both philosophical and practical suggestions for mapping practices and can be a good resource to prepare staff members for mapping sequenced learning. She suggests a mapping process indicating where student learning is introduced (I), reinforced (R), and emphasized (E). This kind of mapping should be an ongoing activity to continually reevaluate integration, redundancy, and gaps. Using Maki's model, with shared goals, educators can look at new-student orientation as a place of *introduction*; residence life, health services, wellness, conduct, student centers, and so on as places of *reinforcement*; and career centers, counseling centers, dean of students, and so on as places where learning is *emphasized*. Table 4.2 offers an example of mapping across departments.

Regardless of institution size or type, student learning does not happen in a bifurcated fashion. Mapping can help us organize our initiatives

TABLE 4.2
Example of Mapping Learning Initiatives Across Departments

Learning outcome (LO): Self-discovery		LO 1 Cultivate curiosity through exploration of new ideas and experiences			LO 2 Develop awareness of individual interests, strengths, and values			LO 3 Develop greater understanding of one's personal identity			LO 4 Draw meaningful connections between identity and purpose		
Career services	Individual appointments	I	R	E	I	R	E	I				R	E
Career services	Workshops	I			I	R	E	I	R		I	R	E
Multicultural life	Intergroup dialogue	I	R	E	I	R		I	R	E	I	R	E
Multicultural life	Leadership retreat	I	R	E	I	R		I	R	E	I	R	E
Orientation	Large sessions	I			I			I			I		
Orientation	Orientation small-group discussions	I	R		I	R		I	R		I		
Orientation	Intentional conversations	I	R	E	I	R	E	I	R		I		

I = introduced, R = reinforced, E = emphasized

across the division in line with the student experience, rather than in line with our established or preferred organizational workflow. Sharing maps with students can help them see intentionality, recognize the progressive nature of their student experience, and make connections that scaffold their own learning. Because maximizing student learning is the priority, it is wise to consider how resources are being used and whether current efforts can realistically contribute to student learning. Having an external facilitator, such as a faculty member from the college of education or from a curriculum design program, could help student affairs educators conduct this mapping and draw conclusions with the help of someone with expertise in this area who does not have an emotional connection to existing strategies. Mapping can also help educators identify strategies to eliminate, or sunset, practices that no longer best support learning aims. The art of letting go of practices that no longer add significant value to student learning is a hallmark of professionalism and fine stewardship of resources and is discussed further in chapter 6.

Facilitation Guides

This component of the curriculum is analogous to lesson plans an elementary teacher would develop or a faculty member would provide to their teaching assistant. *Facilitation guides* and *lesson plans* are used as interchangeable terms for these resources. Facilitation guides are used to guide the implementation of learning strategies. Facilitation guides articulate strategy-level learning outcomes, tied to the broader division- or department-level learning outcomes, and how this learning will be achieved. For example, there could be a facilitation guide for each session during international student orientation and for each activity during the multicultural leadership retreat. Once again, inviting stakeholders, such as faculty from the college of education or a curriculum design program, can be a way to instill a common lens and perspective on facilitation guides as tools when designing and delivering learning strategies.

The level of detail included in a facilitation guide can have a direct correlation to how the learning strategy is delivered. Commonly included details are specifics about timing, the rationale for the strategy, activities, ways of engagement, and assessment. These documents should be detailed in such a manner that a substitute facilitator could be prepared to deliver the learning strategy with limited notice. Facilitation guides should be developed by small teams, and the most educationally sound and practical ideas should be considered such that learning can be facilitated for a broad number of students aligned with the overall learning aims.

Specific strategy-level learning outcomes are directly derived from division or department learning outcomes. If a division learning goal of self-awareness has several division learning outcomes, one of these outcomes might be, "Each student will be able to accurately describe themselves to others." An example of a derived strategy-level learning outcome for intentional one-on-one conversations between paraprofessional staff and students might be, "Each student will be able to articulate four things that make them unique during the intentional conversation." This strategy-level outcome is detailed and specific but still tied to the larger learning aims. Examining ways in which strategy-level outcomes complement or triangulate the depth and breadth of learning opportunities across strategies is critical. Writing facilitation guides should be done after the learning strategies have been identified and the developmental sequencing has been completed, reviewed, reconsidered, and finalized. Getting the sequencing right prevents wasted time writing facilitation guides that may not be used or be used ineffectively.

To write a facilitation guide, begin with the strategy-level learning outcome and work backward to plan the implementation of the strategy. Writing quality strategy-level learning outcomes is key. Using the SWiBAT + Bloom's action verb + condition process will help create consistent learning outcomes across educational plans (Anderson et al., 1994). Once strong, clear, assessable strategy-level learning outcomes that map back to the department or division learning goals and outcomes are in place, writing facilitation guides includes filling in the details of time, location, materials, and activities. A facilitation guide template is shown in Figure 4.3.

Writing detailed facilitation guides is important to advance student learning for several reasons. First, having the guides in place helps ensure that, in different contexts and with different facilitators, similar experiences are being offered, creating a continuity of experience for the learners. Second, guides provide experience fidelity so that when assessed across these different contexts, modifications can confidently be made for improvement. Over the years, a good detailed facilitation guide can be improved over and over as it is fine-tuned based on feedback, diverse thinking, new scholarship, and assessment data. Specific facilitation guides also help when there is staff turnover. The more details that are captured, the less a new staff member must create from scratch and the more they can build on what has already been developed. The opportunities for continuous improvement can be energizing as they help us let go of needing to get things right and be more focused on improving our work for students through revision, innovation, creativity, and engaging with learners themselves to improve the experience for other learners.

Figure 4.3. Facilitation guide template.

1. Details of the strategy:
   a. Title of strategy:
   b. Facilitator(s):
   c. Date/time:
   d. Location:
2. Learning desired:
   a. Division/department learning outcomes:
   b. Strategy-level learning outcomes:
3. Target audience(s):
4. Needed supplies/materials:
5. Outline for implementation:
   a. Step 1:
   b. Step 2:
   c. Step 3:
6. Assessment plan:

Educational Plan Document

Earlier in this chapter, the authors introduced the concept of educational plans. Now, after covering the previous components, this section includes more details about the educational plan document itself. Create a template for educational plans so that there is a consistent structure that can be used in a department or across a division. Taking the time to establish a template that incorporates each component while honoring specific campus or cultural norms is central to creating consistency in delivering the learning. This can be accomplished by a smaller working group within a division or department to afford focused conversation and a reasonable array of ideas. This group of individuals can consider cultural norms about how information is accessed and presented on campus and ways in which this tool can supplement rather than duplicate other tools such as standard operating procedures used for less educationally purposeful activities. The educational plan template can then be vetted by those who will use it to identify questions and points for clarification and to help consider potential additions or changes to the template.

Educational plans typically include the learning aims (educational priority, goals, and outcomes), learners identified (e.g., orientation participants or residents in apartments and suites), and educational strategies and reflect developmental sequencing and facilitation guides. In the educational plan, sequencing chat can also be listed in chronological order with other details. Facilitation guides are sometimes included in the overall educational plan or distributed separately to not overwhelm facilitators. In the latter case, they are distributed to correspond with preplanned facilitator training. Having information in a single document helps to provide guidance and clarity and allows staff to see the interconnections of learning opportunities. Educational plans and facilitation guides are revised regularly, often annually, for continuous improvement.

Assessment Plans

A comprehensive assessment plan helps educators continuously monitor and improve all the components involved in an implemented curricular approach. Assessment can help educators understand the depth and breadth of student demographics, influence facilitation guides, shift developmental sequencing, reconsider selected strategies, and may even inform changes and adjustments to learning aims. Assessment informs decisions about where resources such as time, money, and staffing are best focused to improve learning efforts. Educators should engage in assessment practices that help them determine if students are learning what is espoused in stated aims for student learning and if approaches to facilitating that learning are helping or getting in the way of that learning. Successful student affairs educators use assessment to improve work with students, and celebrating failures equally with successes can be critical in creating a culture of assessment (Gardner, 2016). If assessment indicates that learning goals and outcomes are not being met, it may be because the design of educational efforts or execution of the learning strategies was ineffective. Or, perhaps learning aims were too aspirational or not aspirational enough.

Student affairs educators should become familiar with institutional protocols for assessment, such as coordination of assessment schedules and expectations for use of platforms. Timely and transparent communication across departments can be helpful for reducing duplication of efforts and creating synergy across efforts. Some campuses' institutional review boards (IRBs) require a review for internal assessment projects. Further, a comprehensive plan for assessment can be a useful ongoing communication tool to visualize and commit to ways in which assessment will permeate the design, implementation, and ongoing renewal of all components of the curricular approach. In many ways, such a plan serves to illustrate how pieces of a context (or puzzle pieces) can cast vision and tell a story (a completed puzzle). Taking this analogy one step further, it can be useful to include this content in a chart or spreadsheet. Previously in this chapter, the authors suggested using a chart to depict how the learning goals and outcomes influence the development of educational strategies and how the strategies are sequenced within a time frame. Similarly, the related assessment techniques for each educational strategy can be incorporated to help depict a comprehensive assessment approach.

It is important to avoid making assessment synonymous with surveys. Multiple tools are necessary to measure student learning. Qualitative and quantitative assessment approaches are equally valuable within the curricular approach. Assessment strategies should be simple while providing highly useful information to improve student learning efforts. Assessment strategies may be formative (fostering learning) and summative (summarizing whether learning happened). For example, a program coordinator in the orientation office may ask her student team leader to reflect on her leadership style at the start of the summer and again once orientation has concluded to both understand what growth has occurred in the student and help the student reflect on and acknowledge that growth. Both *Learning Assessment Techniques: A Handbook for College Faculty* (Barkley & Major, 2016) and *Classroom Assessment Techniques: A Handbook for College Teachers* (Angelo & Cross, 1993) provide a wide variety of assessment strategies that are readily applied to learning beyond the classroom.

For one example, students might be asked to use a note card for a "3-2-1" activity (Angelo & Cross, 1993). Facilitators can adopt what the actual prompt may be, but, for example, students who participated in a diversity dialogue may be asked to write three ideas they learned from the conversation, two ways they expect to apply what they learned to their roles as student leaders, and one question or topic they would like to revisit to learn more. A second example might entail asking students to write a statement of their top takeaway from an experience on a whiteboard or large piece of paper. A third example, to promote even more creativity and engagement, would be to give students a specific prompt and ask them to capture photos and write corresponding captions to document their thoughts and experiences. Focus groups, campus-wide surveys, and analysis of existing institutional data may be other assessment strategies helpful in a curricular approach. Grade comparisons, retention and persistence standards, and conduct incidences can also be tracked within a curricular approach.

An inventory of qualitative and quantitative assessment efforts can be developed by using learning goals and learning outcomes as the framework. Such an inventory can help deepen dialogue within a division or department about how distinct efforts can add to both dimensions of assessment. Creating a cycle of assessment can be useful within a division or department to approach assessment such that metrics are used and data collected can inform future direction. For example, cycle of assessment could entail assessing certain learning goals and learning outcomes one year, others the next, and so on in a cyclical manner, or particular strategies this year and others next year. Such an approach may be a useful way to afford time for staff to refocus pedagogy or make adjustments that were otherwise not evident until in use with students. This type of strategic assessment can yield useful results while not overassessing students.

Establishing and committing to review cycles will be helpful to gather insights from those using the facilitation guides, and from students who have participated in learning opportunities. A simple electronic form or shared spreadsheet can be a practical way to capture these ideas. Valuable suggestions emerge to adjust pedagogy and content or to abandon strategies that are not working and replace with better strategies for student learning. Departments and divisions that can commit to regular assessment retreats, assessment poster sessions, and assessment showcases to develop a culture of assessment will have the most success with a curricular approach. Chapter 6 addresses several characteristics for how organizational cultures can be cultivated to embrace ongoing learning in this area.

Continuous Improvement

The design, implementation, and assessment of a curricular approach is never finished. It is an ongoing process of continuous improvement for the betterment of student learning. What educators learn from practice, feedback, assessment, as well as the ways that institutions, students, and the context beyond our institutions change should always be considered and reconsidered. A mind-set of continuous improvement and embracing change and growth can be invaluable for today's student affairs educator. Following, the authors identify four considerations key for the necessary continuous improvement associated with the curricular approach.

The first consideration for continuous improvement is that the *design, implementation, and assessment of the curricular components is cyclical and should be conducted regularly*. Assessment is critical to enhancing student learning and cannot be a task that is completed at the end of the year. A yearlong approach, with techniques mentioned earlier and in the assessment literature at large, is important. Further, assessment findings should be communicated in a transparent and timely manner. For example, a report or infographic on the data and recommendations for practice can be distributed to a variety of stakeholders on a quarterly basis via electronic means and formal and informal meetings. The quality of the components of the curricular approach directly influences the quality of impact on student learning. For example, do assessment results show problems with design or implementation? More proactively, the reader may notice in the description of several components that we suggest day-long or longer workshops or retreats to design or assess the curriculum. Longer reviews might include internal or external reviews. In sum, critical looks at the components, and the synergy among them, are directly proportional to the results that can be achieved for student success.

The second consideration for continuous improvement is to *be specific, integrated, and essential*. Being specific with this work requires concrete and clear guidance for implementation. The design should produce the tools for strategic efforts that contribute to student learning. Being integrated across the student experience means being mindful of the notions of mapping and integration across time, within time, and for different learners. For example, division-wide goals and outcomes can help shape practice such that students' learning builds over time, beginning with participation in orientation to engagement in living and learning communities. Then, first-year students become second-year students and are exposed to a different and progressive host of learning-centered experiences. Integration also applies to collaboration across departments. Real collaboration, not cooperation, can be achieved when partners work together to design learning strategies that can be nimble within the department context but are undergirded by a shared vision for learning goals and learning outcomes. Finally, it is essential to "weed the garden." Freeing the garden of anything that steals nutrients, water, and sunlight from the desired plants or flowers is like removing barriers and obstacles and less powerful initiatives in the curricular journey. For example, making the decision to eliminate paraprofessional staff as designers of door decorations or bulletin boards in residence hall communities can afford more time for them to engage with their peers through meaningful dialogues. Student affairs educators may also consider evaluating and shortening or potentially eliminating certain administrative processes, such as lengthy handwritten forms, as another way to direct more time and energy toward student learning. Student affairs educators who practice essentialism in their curricular approach can ultimately do less so that they can be more for students (McKeown, 2014). Essentialism is discussed further in chapter 6.

The third consideration for continuous improvement is to *be open to a new perspective*. The curricular approach can resemble the clarity of putting on a pair of eyeglasses or feeling the sunshine after a long, harsh winter. Perhaps the most direct way to articulate this new perspective is to view the curricular approach as a transformation, not an add-on to existing practice. Adopting the curricular approach can contribute to increased effectiveness and calls for reevaluating all philosophies and practices that can influence student learning. For example, there is a need for both good customer service and facilitating student learning, but these roles require thoughtful definition and parameters to illustrate that these roles are not always isolated from one another. With this fresh perspective, student affairs educators are better equipped to tell the story of how they are contributing to students' educational experiences at colleges and universities.

The fourth consideration for continuous improvement is to *revisit the entire curriculum as needed*. A periscope is a tool used on submarines to keep an eye on happenings in plain view or on the horizon. With the curricular approach, student affairs educators must constantly maintain perspective on global, national, regional, and institutional arenas. New leadership, new strategic plans, new institutional goals, differences in students attending, revisions to general education requirements, campus climate findings, restructuring of programs and services, and other changes warrant attention and exploration for impacts on the curriculum. For example, the archaeological dig may resemble a "re-dig," resulting in changes and additions or mere confirmation that what is known to support is continually executed and assessed in a similar manner as originally conceived.

Conclusion

In this chapter, the authors described the steps required to design and implement a curricular approach. Whatever an institution designs will be reflected in educational plans that are regularly assessed and revised, so continuous improvement will occur. Each component of a curricular approach is iterative and builds from the last. While the authors describe the process in a linear fashion, it is rarely as direct as explained. The last two chapters of the book describe some pedagogical and leadership considerations that need to be considered as a dynamic and ever-evolving curricular approach is being implemented on any campus.

5

FACILITATING STUDENT LEARNING BEYOND THE CLASSROOM

In the first four chapters of this book, the authors explored the rationale for a curricular approach and described the approach through the 10 essential elements in chapters 1 and 2, respectively. We then presented the key components of a curricular approach and strategies for developing them in chapters 3 and 4. In this chapter, we focus on exploring contemporary understandings of student learning and a broad array of strategies to foster learning beyond the classroom. The paradigms, approaches, and tools discussed here are not prescriptive but offered for student affairs educators to explore as they work to best meet the needs of the unique students, learning aims, and educational plans on their campuses.

If you are asked to close your eyes and remember your own learning moments, chances are you will almost immediately think of a formal classroom learning environment. You may see an instructor delivering a lecture at the front of a large classroom. You may see research papers, group project meetings, math problems, or lab exercises. Images of late nights in a coffee shop studying or writing while sipping a cup of coffee may be part of your memories. As you continue to reflect on learning moments, you may also begin to see other images in your mind such as a residence hall room, a student government association late-night executive board meeting, a fraternity and sorority leadership retreat, or a spring break service-learning trip to Texas. This latter list of memories is of spaces that provide numerous opportunities and potential platforms for learning beyond the classroom environment.

Rethinking Student Affairs Roles as Educators

A curricular approach means thinking of student affairs professionals as educators and reconsidering how work, processes, and initiatives can be learning focused (Whitt, 2006). This may seem like a shift student affairs professional would embrace. Many in student affairs already refer to themselves as "student affairs educators." However, making this shift is more than practitioners superficially changing how they refer to themselves; it is a significant change in how practitioners go about their work. What does it mean to be educators? It requires an understanding of how to best support student learning.

The first step to achieve this understanding is for student affairs educators to critically reflect on current practice and be willing to let go of what they have done in the past, their socialization in the profession, and formal education as student affairs professionals. A curricular approach to student affairs work requires a willingness to unlearn familiar and comfortable approaches and an openness to learning and developing new approaches.

Recently, one of the authors (Knerr) sat down with her grade school–aged child to help her with her math homework. Knerr describes the situation:

> My child was learning division. I sat down and began to show her long division and she looked up at me and said that was wrong. She then showed me the teacher's example. I had no idea what the teacher was doing—only that it was not long division. The teacher came to the same answer that I did, but what was written on the paper was significantly different from how I was taught to do long division. To help my child with her homework, I had to unlearn everything I knew about long division, watch several videos on new math, practice, and then work with my child so that she understood the content.

The same is true for too many student affairs educators. The authors of this book have too often caught ourselves continuing to do the same things with little thought as to whether they work, or we just assume they do work for students. The authors have also heard too often tired, overwhelmed, and burned-out staff members say things like, "If it isn't broken, don't fix it" or, "This is the way we always did it" or, "This is what I did when I was in college." Student affairs educators, like educators of all kinds, too often create opportunities for learning that replicate their own experiences years (or decades) ago as college students. And finally, too often student affairs educators use their own experiences as learners and universalize it and apply the "how I best learn strategy" to others. Intentional reflection and unlearning are critical.

Professional preparation, student affairs socialization, and familiar patterns can lead student affairs educators to unchallenged practice. This practice, in many cases, is based on myths or unfounded but widely held beliefs that guide common practice, maintain the status quo, and reinforce existing systems of inequity in educational practice beyond the classroom. Some of these myths include the following:

- First-year students need extroverted, energized, outgoing resident assistants.
- Students will not come to this or that type of activity.
- Diversity programs reach only those who are already interested in diversity.
- If you do not offer free food, no one will come.
- Proximity to diversity will lead to positive learning outcomes related to diversity.
- Large-scale programs and events are the best way to meet student needs.
- If we provide a buffet of opportunities on campus, students are going to pick learning activities that will challenge themselves and their worldviews in developmentally appropriate ways.

In fact, these statements are not accurate and not good guides for practice. Each myth needs to be carefully reconsidered.

Much of how many student affairs educators were likely taught as students has been disconnected from the newer research from cognitive psychology, neuroscience, and other disciplines on teaching and learning (Fried, 2016) as well as decades of work on critical pedagogy (Freire, 1972/2000; hooks, 1994; Tuitt et al., 2016). In fact, what we now know about learning is often counterintuitive to what we previously thought we knew about learning (P.C. Brown et al., 2014).

As educators let go of some frameworks, they must replace them with more empirically validated and liberatory student learning constructs. Both faculty and educators beyond the classroom have expertise, professors in their discipline and student affairs professionals in student development. Neither group arrives to their role with a high degree of formal training in the art and science of learning. Trial-and-error approaches to improving teaching and learning are not adequate, and all college educators, both within and beyond the classroom, gain from a continued exploration of the processes and products of learning.

Student affairs educators can also learn much from resources outside of traditional higher education literature such as K–12 literature, behavioral economics, leadership, social justice and social change, counseling/psychology, or positive psychology to better understand our current students and what others are saying about how people learn, grow, develop, change, think, practice, play, or are challenged. Student affairs educators need to explore and often adapt strategies from these other areas to better support the learning and growth of all students in higher education.

Facilitating student learning compels student affairs educators to understand neuroscience, content, pedagogy, the educator, and the learner. Educators cannot ask students to go where they are unwilling to go themselves. What content needs to be learned and understood? What pedagogies and new competencies need to be developed? How is the educator's capacity ascertained? Each student affairs educator is neither equipped to educate students on all topics nor competent at using all pedagogies. Participating in an intergroup dialogue on race and ethnicity does not itself prepare someone to facilitate an intergroup dialogue for others. What content about race and ethnicity needs to be learned and unlearned? What about intergroup dialogue needs to be better understood, practiced, and learned? Student affairs leadership needs to be confident their identified educators are prepared and ready to facilitate learning. Where do student staff members need to receive better training to facilitate the content and pedagogy? Where is this unrealistic and professional staff responsible for this learning? Where are expectations of professional staff unrealistic and where are campus or community partners engaged to best foster student learning and avoid harm?

In addition to building educator competencies, the best student affairs educators view themselves as scholar-practitioners. To fully center student learning in student affairs practice, key elements of the work must focus on ongoing explorations of teaching and learning. This means intentional time in schedules to think about learning and reflection, to study how students best engage with and learn new material, and to practice learning-centered approaches. This implies significant refocusing of things such as professional development, credentialing, and core competencies of a successful student affairs educator. Centering practices on student learning also evolves the scope of student affairs partnerships into areas such as faculty teaching and enrichment centers or in education academic departments.

What Is Learning?

Cognitive psychology and neuroscience have helped us better understand what learning is as a process (P.C. Brown et al., 2014; Fried, 2016). Ambrose et al. (2010) describe learning as the following:

1. Learning is a *process,* not a product.
2. Learning involves *change* in knowledge, beliefs, behaviors, or attitudes. Learning is not something done *to* students, but rather something students do (p. 3).

Additionally, Lang (2016) describes in his book *Small Teaching* three parts of learning:

1. Knowledge: Retrieving, predicting, and interleaving
2. Understanding: Connecting, practicing, and self-explaining
3. Inspiration: Motivating, growing, and expanding

Bloom's (1956) taxonomy, now revised (Anderson et al., 1994), as well as Fink's (2013) significant learning experiences, offer ways to conceptualize the increasing levels of cognitive complexity of different forms of learning. The use of a taxonomy offers the designer of a learning experience a model of effective starting points and the progression of the learning building blocks. Aspiring educators must avoid the temptation to immediately aim for the top of the pyramid and recognize the value of the base of the pyramid as the foundation for higher level learning, thinking, and application. As P.C. Brown et al. (2014) explain, "Pitting the learning of basic knowledge against the development of creative thinking is a false choice" (p. 30). Willingham (2009) further explains, "Research from cognitive science has shown that the sorts of skills that teachers want for their students—such as the ability to analyze and think critically—require extensive factual knowledge" (p. 25).

Types of Learning

Scholars have outlined different types of learning. These types describe different ways of thinking about learning, but they are not mutually exclusive and may overlap. Expanding the ways we understand learning can only expand our ability to foster student learning. Knowledge learning is perhaps the most familiar type of learning. This is learning to retain information into memory. It is also the foundation of more complex ways of learning. All learning requires memory, at least at its foundation (P.C. Brown et al., 2014).

Baxter Magolda and King (2004) portray a more complex view of learning with their "three core assumptions about learning: knowledge is complex and socially constructed, one's identity plays a central role in crafting knowledge claims, and knowledge is mutually constructed via the sharing of expertise and authority" (p. xix). Fried (2016) adds that we must expand the concept of self beyond the individualized self to also include the collective self.

Another type of learning is mindful learning or contemplative-based learning practices (Barbezat & Bush, 2014). Langer (1997) describes mindful learning as "the continuous creation of new categories, openness to new information, and an implicit awareness of more than one perspective" (p. 4). Berila (2016) applies these contemplative or mindfulness-based approaches specifically to anti-oppression education and teaching for social justice. Ashlee (2017) describes using mindfulness approaches to foster racial identity development in White students.

And perhaps the most complex learning is transformative learning, which is learning to transform not just *what* we know but *how* we know in order to shift to our worldview and perspective. Mezirow (2000) explains,

> Transformative learning refers to the process by which we transform our taken-for-granted frames of reference (meaning perspectives, habits of mind, mind-sets) to make them more inclusive, discriminating, open, emotionally capable of change, and reflective so that they may generate beliefs and opinions that will prove more true or justified to guide action. (pp. 7–8)

Transformational educators want to support learners' ability to explore who they are in terms of value, purpose, and identity. Kegan (2000) terms this type of learning *self-authorship*.

It is important to recognize these different types of learning and to connect the most apt approach to both the learner and the teaching goal. For example, the teaching techniques focused on memory and content knowledge will certainly be different from those employed to challenge certain habits of mind and introduce others for learners' consideration. A learner-centered approach focuses on the type of learning learners need, not what type of learning educators are most interested in facilitating.

The Neuroscience of Learning

Recent neuroscience has taught us about how the process of learning works in the brain (Siegel, 2010), understanding how the brain processes learning can help us be better learners and better facilitate learning (Bresciani Ludvik, 2016). In fact, conceptualizing how the brain works can help us engage our brain in different ways, a concept Siegel (2010) called *mindsight*. What we are learning about neurogenesis (making new brain cells) and neuroplasticity (making new connections between brain cells) has implications for how educators structure, organize, sequence, and facilitate learning beyond the classroom (Bresciani Ludvik, 2016). Learning is about connections between brain cells. The more often educators make these connections, the more long term the learning will be. Educators can help learners use practice, focus, attention, and effort to reinforce, strengthen, and make those connections second nature (Doyle & Zakrajsek, 2018). Educators can help students learn skills like attention regulation, emotional regulation, and cognitive regulation with tools such as reflection and mindfulness to enhance well-being, resilience, creativity, compassion, empathy, integration, and critical thinking (Bresciani Ludvik, 2016).

Siegel (2010) explains that the brain is an organ between your ears, but the mind is the interconnection of the brain and body with signals going from not only the brain to the body (Pick that up) but also the body to the brain (I feel queasy on this amusement park ride). This is part of the reason why fostering well-being is such a key part of facilitating learning. Neuroscience has shown us that sleep, rest, nutrition, and exercise support and prepare us for learning (Doyle & Zakrajsek, 2018) and are critical to the actual learning process (McGuire & McGuire, 2018). Cramming, multitasking, and stress all inhibit learning, while breaks, emotional connection, and positive emotions enhance learning (Doyle & Zakrajsek, 2018).

Here are a few key insights aggregated from neuroscience for fostering learning (Bresciani Ludvik, 2016; Doyle & Zakrajsek, 2018; Jensen, 2008; Medina, 2014; Siegel, 2010; Zadina, 2014):

1. Engage all the senses.
2. Engage the mind (knowing), heart (emotions), and body (movement).
3. Foster well-being for the body and mind with sleep, rest, nutrition, hydration, and exercise.
4. Support learners in managing stress, threats, oppression, and fear, and don't add to them.
5. Foster intrinsic motivation through meaning, relevance, and rigor, and by celebrating progress.
6. Encourage focused attention (mindfulness, not multitasking) in short spurts with lots of breaks.
7. Encourage doing and reflecting in an ongoing cycle.
8. Cultivate positive emotions and social connections.

None of these insights are represented in the business-as-usual approach of a lecture- and slides-based workshop inside or beyond the classroom.

The Learning Process

The learning process is complex, including how we learn; how we retain what we learned; and the role of unlearning, connecting motivation, and learning about learning. In their 2014 book *Make It Stick*, P.C. Brown et al. (2014) explain the learning process as retrieval, effort, and interleaving. Engaging prior knowledge is key to all learning (P.C. Brown et al., 2014). Connecting new learning to prior knowledge is how learning works (Doyle & Zakrajsek, 2018). In fact, the common phrase "meet students where they are" can be best operationalized through the process of connecting new learning to student prior knowledge, including student misconceptions of knowledge. Retrieving information is better at fostering learning than repeated consuming of information, such as repeated reading. Repeated retrieval that is challenging (effort) and spaced out (interleaving) is the difference between learning and mindless recitation (P.C. Brown et al., 2014) and "can so embed knowledge and skills that they become reflexive: the brain acts before the mind has time to think" (p. 29).

Motivation is key to learning. It is key to effort, retention, connection, and more. Fried (2016) summarizes one of the biggest learnings from recent cognitive psychology and neuroscience as follows: "It turns out that people learn only what they care about, subjects that have personal meaning for them and are in some way related to their own lives beyond the classroom" (pp. xxvi–xxvii). Intrinsic motivation (finding value in the material or the challenge of learning) is a far better motivator than extrinsic motivations (money, status, or grades) (Ambrose et al., 2010). "Learning is stronger when it matters, when the abstract is made concrete and personal" (P.C. Brown et al., 2014, p. 11). At times, this means that educators must include engaging in a process to help students recognize the value of the subject matter beyond the classroom.

Unlearning is harder than learning. Learning new information simply includes encoding, retaining, and applying. Unlearning requires a much more complex process of engaging and conflicting with prior knowledge (Ambrose et al., 2010). This is especially true the more deeply the prior learning has been engrained. This a powerful challenge, especially for educators beyond the classroom, where often the primary task is unlearning. For example, it is challenging to unlearn oppressive socialization that is often deeply internalized; unlearn harmful patterns of dealing with conflict from years of immersion in unhealthy family dynamics; or unlearn unhealthy behaviors engrained through inaccurate information, peer influence, and/or addictions.

TABLE 5.1
Metacognition

Unconscious incompetence	I don't know that I don't know how to tie my shoes.
Conscious incompetence	I don't know how to tie my shoes. Help me?
Conscious competence	I know how to tie my shoes!
Unconscious competence	I tie my shoes every day, and I don't consciously know how I tie my shoes.

Metacognition is literally how one thinks about thinking, learning, and understanding. Understanding how we learn and being able to adjust our learning efforts help us become less passive and more proactive (McGuire & McGuire, 2018). With metacognition, learners evaluate their problem-solving and reflect on their depth of learning to become more empowered learners. Self-reflection seems easy but can be a bit more complicated. Johari's window applied to knowing and competence (Howell & Fleishman, 1982) can be a useful example of metacognition, as outlined in Table 5.1.

The aspects of the learning process just discussed are summarized into actionable chunks (a tool to help make complex information more retainable) by Ambrose et al. (2010) in their book *How Learning Works: Seven Research-Based Principles for Smart Teaching*.

1. "Students' prior knowledge can help or hinder learning" (p. 4).
2. "How students organize knowledge influences how they learn and apply what they know" (p. 4).
3. "Students' motivation determines, directs, and sustains what they do to learn" (p. 5).
4. "To develop mastery, students must acquire component skills, practice integrating them, and know when to apply what they have learned" (p. 5).
5. "Goal-directed practice coupled with targeted feedback enhances the quality of students' learning" (p. 5).
6. "Students' current level of development interacts with the social, emotional, and intellectual climate of the course to impact learning" (p. 6).
7. "To become self-directed learners, students must learn to monitor and adjust their approaches to learning" (p. 6).

Learners benefit from learning about the learning process. Good educators help students understand how learning works, teach students how to learn, create "just right" difficulties and challenges in the learning environment to foster learning, and are transparent about how they are facilitating the learning process (P.C. Brown et al., 2014). By learning about the components of the learning process students are better and more empowered learners. This also helps them transfer these skills beyond the content, skill, or task before them and apply it to future tasks as well. This not only is good facilitation of learning but also cultivates effective lifelong learners who will be able to learn knowledge that does not exist today.

In higher education, many student affairs educators try to address real problems such as student depression, anxiety, oppression, lack of resources, social isolation, alcohol and drug use, stress, and more. These are real issues students face that do need to be addressed. But as Seligman (2011) points out, educators are likely to be more successful in direct approaches (teaching well-being and learning strategies) rather than indirect approaches (helping students overcome and recover from academic failure, mental illness, substance abuse, etc.) to student success. Rather than anticipate what could sabotage student success and try to prevent it, what about teaching students how to learn, be resilient, develop healthy relationships, engage in communities, and have greater openness to diversity? Changes in behavior, resilience, and perspectives depend on learning new areas of knowledge, new skills, and new habits of mind. A centered focus on student learning and student affairs teaching methods may be the most effective route to helping students as they face these real challenges.

Research has shown that fostering your well-being, knowing your strengths and using them more often, being kind, expressing gratitude, seeking social support, and practicing meditation are beneficial for student learning and student success (Achor, 2010; Fredrickson, 2012; Seligman, 2011). Good pedagogy would include teaching these approaches in orientation, workshops, social media campaigns, and peer education.

Educators working with a curricular approach must believe in and help students develop a growth mind-set. Having a growth mind-set can help students advance their learning (Dweck, 2008). Individuals with a fixed mind-set see intelligence as static. They seek to prove they are smart by avoiding challenges, give up in the face of obstacles, see effort as a sign of failure, avoid negative feedback, and resent the success of others. Individuals with a growth mind-set see learning as a process. This fosters a desire to learn by seeking challenges, persist through setbacks, view effort as a path to mastery, learn from criticism, and find lessons and inspiration in the success of others. Many students have a fixed mind-set based on feedback about their intelligence (often the most privileged) or lack of intelligence (often the most marginalized and minoritized). As educators explicitly explaining growth mind-set, its benefits to learning and success, and encouraging growth mind-set through our approaches and feedback with students can foster learning, growth, and success within current systems and structures while seeking to create more equitable and just structures on campus and beyond.

Who Are the Learners?

All educators make certain assumptions about the learner in order to design the appropriate content and educational experiences. When working one-on-one in a teaching/learning environment, it may be easier to explore social group identities, institutional roles, prior knowledge, and so on. When working on a workshop for 12 students, a retreat for 75, or an orientation session for 900, broader institution studies of students (first generation? adult learners?) or national trend analysis reports can be helpful in determining both starting points and learning process stages.

Today, college students are changing and have different needs than previous groups of learners (Almanac, 2017; Bill and Melinda Gates Foundation, 2018; Renn & Reason, 2013). Students of color are nearly half (45.2%) of undergraduates in the United States (Espinosa et al., 2019). There has been tremendous growth in nontraditional student populations. More students are coming to college after active military service, demographics of international students are changing, and more students are coming to college with significant mental health challenges. And these are just some of the changes that are occurring. We may also be seeing these trends differently on our individual campuses, with some seeing greater shifts and others less change.

As the iGen (those born in the mid-90s to early 2010s) enters higher education, educators are beginning to see students entering college who have always had mobile technology in their hands (Twenge, 2017). They have never experienced dial-up Internet and have always had Netflix and a cell phone. For many of them, their textbook and educational content has almost always been delivered electronically via a laptop computer. They have grown up in the age of social media with accounts on Facebook, Twitter, Instagram, and Snapchat. They have experienced bullying online; they communicate via text messages and emojis. Despite being constantly immersed and surrounded by technology, they can be technology dependent rather than technology savvy. As a result, some students struggle with interpersonal communication, formal language writing, and resolving conflict (Twenge, 2017). They are willing to put in long hours and work hard. As these students begin to enter higher education, educators are quickly seeing that they communicate, learn, and think very differently than millennials. To help them make meaning of their college experience and help them achieve learning goals, educators need to design learning experiences differently to meet the new generation's unique needs and perspectives (Twenge, 2017).

Good educators are also working hard to be more conscious of their own implicit bias (Banaji & Greenwald, 2013) and to counter assumptions and stereotypes they may have about students. While it is useful to have general information about a generation of students, populations such as African American students, first-generation students, or veterans, getting to know an individual and their personal story will always allow for the best educational experience. Student affairs educators must be committed to suspending assumptions, developing their own critical consciousness, and working with students to challenge the systemic barriers within and beyond institutions of higher education (Quaye et al., 2018).

Critical Perspective on Knowledge, Learning, and Pedagogy

Pedagogy is how we facilitate the process of learning (Fried, 2016). In the same way that the theoretical frames on the learning process are too complex to present beyond a simple introduction in this text, pedagogy is similarly complex in its range of theoretical frames. It is, however, essentially important to the learning process and the design of the educational experience. Defining pedagogy as how educators facilitate learning is very different from defining it as how we teach. Student affairs educators want a learner-centered approach to educating beyond the classroom. Good pedagogy is based on not only personal experience but also on scholarship, including empirical evidence and clear conceptual and theoretical thinking. It is applying what we know about learning and learners. There are various pedagogical approaches and strategies for educators to utilize beyond the classroom. Those discussed here are the ones the authors have used or observed to be used in guiding curricular design beyond the classroom. We encourage readers to explore the approaches deeper by referring to the texts cited.

Knowledge is socially constructed (Baxter Magolda & King, 2004) and thus so is learning and pedagogy. Further, knowledge, learning, and pedagogy are socially constructed in social systems that are inequitable and unjust at the individual, institutional, and societal level (Adams & Zuniga, 2016). Critical theorists in education such as Bell (1992), Freire (1972/2000), hooks (1994), Giroux (2011), Delgado and Stefancic (2017), and others have outlined how educational systems not only are a result of systems of oppression but also can replicate, reinforce, and perpetuate systems of oppression. Systems of power and oppression impact how and what we learn, what knowledge is valued, and what ways of learning are privileged (Patel, 2016; Tuitt et al., 2016). Without intentional and repeated efforts to be mindful and conscious of these social inequities along the lines of race, gender, class, ability, religion, citizenship status, gender identity, sexual orientation, age, and more (Adams & Zuniga, 2016), educators will not only fail in reducing the impact of oppression and privilege that students experience in the learning environment but also actively contribute to it. Educators often reinforce systems of oppression in ways that they are unaware and unconscious of due to their internalized socialization, their internalized dominance or internalized oppression, and the intersections of these systems (Harro, 2000).

Curricular approaches are an opportunity to make the content and the process of learning explicit, which opens the teaching and learning to critique, assessment, and revision from a critical, inclusive, and social justice lens. A traditional programming approach is also a dominant approach as it maintains the status quo, because the content and pedagogy are unexamined and most often unstated for learners or for colleagues to question or improve. By making the content and the pedagogy explicit from the beginning, student affairs educators can challenge themselves to be critically conscious in the design, implementation, and assessment of the curriculum. They can also recognize that complete critical consciousness is elusive, and they can continue to invite feedback, input, and partnership with those who may not be represented in the curriculum design process. Creating systems of accountability is key to the curricular approach, as outlined in essential element 9: *A curricular approach is developed through a review process.* Creating systems of accountability that do not replicate systems of oppression by placing the burden to prevent this on members of oppressed, marginalized, and minoritized groups is a challenge itself (Edwards, 2006).

Critical and inclusive pedagogy (Tuitt et al., 2016) includes reexamining, through a social justice lens, how educators think about pedagogy, how they utilize pedagogy, and how they measure impact. Critical and inclusive pedagogy will help student affairs educators examine learning itself, assess a variety of pedagogical approaches, and determine which pedagogical tools can best support students' learning and unlearning. Critical and inclusive pedagogy is liberatory pedagogy (Love, 2000) in that it helps educators focus the design, implementation, and assessment of liberatory pedagogies in their unique curriculum in a way that most benefits those who are most marginalized but still benefits all students. This can help students learn about who they are (identity); who we are (diversity); and the focus of the learning (content) whether it is communication, conflict, self-awareness, communication across difference, or equity and justice (Tuitt et al., 2016). Critical and inclusive pedagogies might include intergroup dialogue, critical self-reflection, community-based learning, service-learning, and critical analysis. However, critical and inclusive pedagogies are not limited to these practices. Other pedagogical strategies listed in this chapter could be used to foster inclusive and social justice–oriented learning depending on if, when, with whom, and how they are facilitated.

No educator is immune to the systems of power, privilege, and oppression. Curricular approaches cannot be created outside of these systems. Those who engage in curriculum development with explicit, intentional, and continued attention to their critical consciousness and how their own biases around content and learning around issues of power, privilege, and oppression of all kinds are likely to do it better than those with no consciousness (Patel, 2016). A curricular approach can be designed with an aspiration for universal design that will work for all learners, especially the most marginalized. However, given the complexity of systemic socialization and the human complexity of teaching and learning, arriving and fully realizing this aspiration across all forms of identity and oppression is likely unreasonable and unrealistic even for the most sophisticated, critically educated, and advanced pedagogical experts. Keeping identity-affirming, equitable, and justice-oriented learning at the center of curricular approaches is a goal to strive for rather than a reality to expect to ever fully achieve in perpetuity (Tuitt et al., 2016). Indeed, the learning and unlearning continues for us all.

Critical pedagogy is very useful for educators facilitating learning through the student experience because of its attention to power (Brookfield, 2000). Freire's (1972/2000) *pedagogy of the oppressed* and hooks's (1994) *engaged pedagogy* are two very useful conceptual models for application in student affairs work. Andragogy, or pedagogy for adult learners, is another useful conceptual model for college students of all ages as well as for staff development and training in a curricular approach (Merriam & Bierema, 2014). These approaches overlap and can be used to complement each other to meet the needs of varied learners or to be appropriately matched with content or process.

Critical pedagogy is more than just theorizing an ideal but working in praxis with teachers and learners together to improve teaching, learning, and liberation. *Advancing Social Justice* by Davis and Harrison (2013) explores pedagogy, tools, and strategies related to social justice education. Chavez and Longerbeam (2016) offer great conceptual grounding as well as pragmatic and practical considerations and recommendations in their book *Teaching Across Cultural Strengths*. Student affairs educators can also return to the scholarship of K–12 education and learn from scholars of culturally relevant teaching (Ladson-Billings, 1994), such as hip-hop pedagogy (Emdin, 2016; Hill, 2009; Love, 2019), and consider the relevant applications for the unique students in their campus environments. Other pedagogies explore indigenous ways of knowing, being, and doing (Smith, 2012; Wilson, 2008).

Rendón (2009) describes a pedagogical approach rooted in hooks's (1994) engaged pedagogy, contemplative pedagogies, relationship-centered approaches, and integrative learning to outline a teaching and learning approach based on "wholeness, harmony, social justice, and liberation" (p. 132). Rendón (2009) calls

> to all those spiritual warriors embarking on this journey: Let us breathe through the cracks of our open hearts. And may our collective breath be the vision of a transformative dream of education that speaks the language of heart and mind and the truth of wholeness, harmony, social justice, and liberation. (p. 151)

Barbezat and Bush (2014) outline the goals of contemplative pedagogy as the following:

1. Focus and attention building, mainly through focusing meditation and exercises that support mental stability
2. Contemplation and introspection into the content of the course, in which students discover the material in themselves and thus deepen their understanding of the material
3. Compassion, connection to others, and a deepening sense of the moral and spiritual aspect of education
4. Inquiry into the nature of their minds, personal meaning, creativity, and insight (p. 11)

Contemplative pedagogy merges 3,000-year-old tradition and wisdom across religious traditions with practices that align with the latest neuroscience on learning (Bresciani Ludvik, 2016). Mindfulness, engaging the senses, embodied learning, deep listening, aligned action, and relational inquiry are all roots of many contemplative practices that are in alignment with the neuroscience of learning research of the past 15 years.

Learning around diversity, equity, inclusion, and social justice are common learning goals beyond the classroom as diversity and inclusion are often institutional priorities. How these goals are defined through the narrative and learning outcomes varies greatly. There is scholarship around the content and the process of social justice education. *Teaching for Diversity and Social Justice* (Adams et al., 2016) provides an excellent foundation, conceptual grounding, and pedagogical considerations for social justice in general and social justice topics specifically. The companion book, *Readings for Diversity and Social Justice* (Adams et al., 2018), is also a great source for content for student learning and professional development.

As a good example of integration and overlap of these pedagogical approaches, Berila (2016) applies these contemplative practices specifically to antioppression and social justice pedagogy. Berila discussed the alignment of feminist and social justice theory and pedagogy with contemplative practices and educational approaches to mitigate the harm of oppression, better foster learning, and more effectively address social justice in the world.

Pedagogical Strategies

Within the many broad pedagogical approaches are a variety of concrete and specific pedagogical strategies. Again, these strategies are not mutually exclusive or the "right" strategies for a curricular approach to student learning beyond the classroom. These are strategies that the authors have used or seen others use successfully. These strategies can be used across the student experience and can be tied to a variety of different learning goals and outcomes. We share these with the hope that they will instigate and fuel innovative thinking. A list of these strategies appears in Appendix K.

Backward Design

In backward design (Wiggins & McTighe, 2005), the educator begins with the end in mind (learning goals and outcomes) and carefully considers what strategies and approaches allow students to achieve the intended outcome. Once the learning is determined, student experiences are identified that will provide opportunities for students to reach that learning goal.

Experiential Learning

As educators intentionally design learning experiences, they must carefully consider how learning occurs. Kolb's (1984) experiential learning model describes four stages for learning to occur. In the first stage, students need an opportunity to have a concrete experience with the material. In the second stage the learner has an opportunity to reflect on the activity. In the third stage the learner moves on to an abstract conceptualization. It is here that they internalize the experience and reflect on it to make their own sense of the learning and begin to explore ways in which it extends abstractly to other areas of their learning, growth, development, or practice. In the fourth stage students integrate their learning and practice or apply it to other areas or experiences. Educators designing learning experiences should consider how to develop or plan opportunities for students to work through all four of these stages.

Learning Partnerships

Learning should be developed as a partnership between the educator and the learner. Baxter Magolda (2001) utilizes a tandem bike metaphor to explain what this might look like. With some educational opportunities, students are sitting in the front—the captain's seat—directing their own learning and educators are in the back contributing, peddling, providing support and additional balance as the students work to create their knowledge. At times, the educator may need to start out in the front, guiding the direction of learning, but encouraging students to take responsibility for their own learning. With a curricular approach, educators with the necessary expertise take responsibility for designing and building the tandem bike and are in constant consideration of where the learner should be and where the educator should be on the bike to best facilitate learning.

The principles to remember with learning partnerships (Baxter Magolda & King, 2004) are (a) validating learners as knowers, (b) situating learning in the learner's own context, and (c) defining learning as mutually constructed learning. For example, in a student conduct meeting the educator could take the approach of simply rearticulating the policies that were violated, advising the student to not repeat the behavior in the future, and giving the student a consequence such as a fine or administrative sanction. However, using the learning partnerships model (Baxter Magolda & King, 2004), a conduct officer would instead use a different, more theoretically informed strategy for learning. In this approach, the conduct officer may share the incident report with the student and then help the student come to an understanding of the decisions that led to this behavior, starting with an exploration of how the student conceptualizes community and how the behavior adversely impacted the individual and the community, and work with the student to identify strategies the student may use to react differently in the future. In this approach, the conduct officer is collaborating with the student to facilitate learning. The conduct officer may ask guiding questions; help the student reflect; and ask questions that cause the student to examine their processes and create a new understanding of the policy, its rationale, and the need for a successful community.

Peer Education

Being asked to explain concepts to peers is a powerful learning strategy (P.C. Brown et al., 2014; Lang, 2016). Peer education can be incorporated into formal programs such as through health and wellness peer educators, orientation leaders, or student organization assistants. It can also be incorporated as a strategy within many different learning contexts. For instance, having participants explain sustainability to their partner in their own words at the end of a workshop can help with knowledge retention. Having students in an alcohol workshop share with their peers information about the biphasic curve and how they plan to use this information can help in retention of information and increase the likelihood of behavior change.

Active Learning

Engaging learners in learning opportunities throughout their student experience requires drawing students into meaningful experiences that challenge their thinking, allowing for opportunities to practice in brave spaces (Arao & Clemens, 2013), and providing opportunities for authentic discussion and feedback. Each unit in student affairs has a variety of administrative processes that create ample opportunities for active learning. Imagine the learning that can occur in engaging in a housing contract process (decision-making and consequences), visiting the health center (learning how to be a consumer in a health-care system/self-advocacy), completing a financial aid loan workshop (practical competence), or registering for the student resource fair (identity). These seemingly tedious administrative processes can often be reimagined into rich learning experiences for students engaging with our offices and resources.

Real-World Learning

In an authentic learning strategy (Herrington & Herrington, 2006), real-world situations are utilized to create opportunities for students to practice skills in new and meaningful ways. Service or community-based learning opportunities are examples of where this can take place. When students engage in community organizations, they can practice a variety of skills such as communication, organization, commitment, supervision, conflict resolution, and global perspective-building. For example, students may engage in making the case for securing and then operating a food pantry on campus. As they navigate to find and operationalize a solution to this problem, they can practice real-world skills with appropriate support in a somewhat structured learning environment. There are numerous real problems facing students, campus communities, institutions, and local or international communities that they can take on rather than pretend to address hypothetical ones.

By practicing skills in real-world situations, students can better develop a sense of professional or social responsibility. It also helps them to see themselves as professionals, problem solvers, and contributing members of communities. Using real-world challenges allows students to explore how to apply their newly developed skills in a variety of situations and provides opportunity to reflect on their own learning. It also provides students with opportunities to not only fail and learn resilience and persistence but also celebrate real successes that build confidence and commitment

Problem-Based Learning

Problem-based learning (PBL) is related to, if not a full actualization of, real-world learning. Traditional methods of knowledge transfer from expert to student have much less relevance in a world where students have vast access to ever-expanding information and knowledge. It is also possible that scientific and technical advances along with rapidly changing businesses and economies outpace the pace of knowledge transfer during the college years. Knowing the right questions to ask, the best sources of information to seek out, and how to apply solutions to a certain context allow us to keep pace with an increasingly complex world.

In *The Power of Problem-Based Learning*, Dutch et al. (2001) describe that within problem-based approaches

> complex, real-world problems are used to motivate students to identify and research the concepts and principles they need to know to work through those problems. Students work in small learning teams, bringing collective skill at acquiring, communicating, and integrating information. (p. 6)

PBL approaches are typically used with small team groups who are presented with a problem. The team identifies gaps between what information they currently possess related to the problem and what information they need to obtain, taking some care not to overwhelm the process by an unattainable list. The team process continues while group members attempt to fill these knowledge gaps, adding to the full team knowledge along the way to the proposed solution.

In larger settings, PBL approaches may be scaled up with more complex (and real) problems that can be portioned for smaller groups to tackle and then bring back to reintegrate into the broader issues at hand. PBL approaches are not typically brief interventions or simple portions of workshops. The problems should be relevant enough to provide effective motivation for the learners, and relevant problems need an appropriate amount of time and opportunity to revisit on multiple occasions. In the classroom, student groups may spend an entire semester on a single problem. Educators beyond the classroom are not likely to have that level of time with students but can still develop team learning experiences using PBL with two to three shorter term gathering opportunities or use the approach throughout a full- or half-day experience such as a retreat or a staff or student leadership training experience.

Critical Reflection

Engaging in critical reflection may seem inescapable and a core part of the human experience. But not all self-reflection fosters learning and growth in ways that benefit the student or contribute to the learning goals and outcomes identified. How do educators engage students in critically examining the assumptions about how the world works, expectations of what will happen, and conclusions about why things happen (Brookfield, 2000)?

Facilitation of critical reflection requires training and practice. Opportunities to integrate well-designed critical reflection into student experiences could include intentional conversations in orientation, retreats for student government leaders, postworkshop debriefs for multicultural assistants, or discussions about conflict at an internship. The right questions and a deep listener can help students gain significant insight into their experiences. This can be facilitated in groups as well.

Freire (1972/2000) discussed the importance of integrating action (practice) and reflection as praxis. Paired together, action and reflection are powerful. Separately they can have limited usefulness or create harm. Some of us love to execute and get things done, but if educators jump into doing without carefully considering what they are doing and how, they can engage in useless action or do real harm. Similarly, some educators love to reflect, think, and critique, but if all they do is engage in this reflection without trying to improve action it can be self-involved and damaging. Educators need to pair action with reflection and not just once but in a continuous cycle. This doing paired with thinking engages multiple cognitive activities and is a powerful learning strategy (P.C. Brown et al., 2014).

Assessment as Pedagogical Strategy

Assessment is a critical part of a curricular approach. Educators need to know what students are learning and if what they are doing is helping or hindering that learning. But assessment need not just be something done at the end to see if it worked or not; assessment can be done throughout a learning experience to instigate and reinforce learning. For example, one might do an anonymous poll about the experiences of sexual violence at the beginning of an orientation session to ground the learning, let survivors know they are not alone, and reinforce the seriousness of the topic for those who may not enter the space with much seriousness. Or, a student affairs educator may ask students to summarize the campus conduct policies in their own words on a note card to not only help assess their effectiveness but also reinforce the learning by asking the students to retrieve the information and elaborate on it in their own words.

Utilizing Technological Tools

Technology has presented a new playground of learning moments and opportunities that can be intentionally tweaked and developed to foster student learning. Utilizing technology such as online instant technology polls, online journals, texting, and social media platforms provides opportunities for students to explore their learning, practice new skills, and make learning connections in new and meaningful ways. Evolving practices in online and distance learning may provide strong new ways to connect with more students in their increasingly complex lives.

For example, student affairs educators might consider using an online polling tool in areas like the dining hall, new student orientation, or career fairs to help students explore their own thoughts around topics; learn from other participants; and reflect on integrating what they said, what others said, and what they want to do related to their own learning and behaviors. Educators can carefully design questions that are displayed throughout a presentation while students are waiting in line for food or while they are putting their coats on after the career fair. These quick learning moments allow for real-time assessment and learning.

Other technology that needs to be considered are social media platforms such as Pinterest, Instagram, Facebook Live, or other social media or online platforms. Use of videos, sound bites, infographics, and posts allows students to think, react, reflect, and integrate action in ways that are different from traditional approaches to teaching in student affairs. For example, showing a quick, humorous video at the first community meeting showing the downfalls of not establishing roommate expectations may allow students to reflect on their conflict styles and the ways in which they set, enforce, and demonstrate expectations and responsibilities in their living environment. A university Pinterest board on respectful demonstrations might encourage reflection on how students are engaging in respective discourse in their campus community. The uses of social media platforms to provide opportunities for student learning are endless.

Intentional Learning Spaces

Intentionally designing physical spaces on campus to align with learning goals can be a pedagogy in and of itself. Meaning-making centers, engagement centers, and maker spaces are some examples of this kind of design.

In Nash and Jang's (2013) *About Campus* article, "The Time Has Come to Create Meaning-Making Centers on College Campuses," the authors call for meaning-making centers as places on campus that are designed specifically to connect educators with students to contextualize learning experiences to deal with the universal, existential questions of life. In these centers, students can connect the dots of their learning around big life questions such as "Who am I?" or "What is my purpose?" Meaning-making centers seek to help students utilize campus curriculum and services to answer these questions. One approach a meaning-making center may take is to create affinity groups for students where they can talk about the big life questions in a brave space (Arao & Clemens, 2013). Other services that the meaning-making center offers would be to help students connect with resources as they process through these life meanings. The goal of meaning-making centers is to create self-aware, self-resolved, globally competent students (Nash & Jang, 2013). Meaning-making centers force collaborations among faculty, staff, administrators, and students as they work together to explore and make connections among the big questions in life, the academic curriculum, and the experiences and resources offered on campus.

Others have used a similar idea to focus resources on specific locations and staff to assist students in engaging in their communities. Engagement centers are spaces, often managed by student affairs staff in central campus locations, that are multifunctional. They might be used for study hours, yoga classes, tutoring, or workshops depending on the time of year and prevailing student needs. Because of their central location, students can readily access a variety of campus resources across a division and beyond student affairs.

Maker spaces designed to foster creativity and innovation are popping up in libraries, residence halls, and other places on campus. Art studios, demonstration kitchens, or 3D printing labs can all align with learning goals related to creativity and innovation.

Innovate Your Own Pedagogical Strategies

The possibilities are limitless. Educators need to be constantly scanning the horizon to find and implement strategies that meet students where they are and for who they may become. They need to encourage innovation. In developing learning strategies, educators often go back to what they are already doing or what worked in the past. Just because it has always been done or because it worked in the past does not mean it is the best approach for our learners currently. Think about what strategies, approaches, and activities could best help students achieve the learning goals set forth by the curricular approach. Take risks, try something new, or be different if you think it will best accomplish the goals to maximize students' learning. Look to trending strategies in K–12 education to see what may be new or innovative to your students.

Conclusion

The discussion in this chapter is intended to introduce a range of perspectives about educators, learners, and potential ways of thinking about and introducing learning. Each section could be a career-long exploration on its own. No educator will be versed in all areas of worthy consideration, but a quality educator utilizes perspectives like those introduced in this chapter to articulate their own philosophy of learning. It is through a comprehensive expression of one's philosophy about the process of learning that the educator can begin to add layers such as those described in this chapter.

Rethinking roles and engaging in a process of unlearning while simultaneously learning new constructs starts with examining current beliefs, values, and paradigms about the process of teaching and learning and then comparing them to new and competing constructs. Expanding consideration about the types of learning, contemporary views about the neuroscience of learning, and the learning process itself will begin the cycle and allow us to begin tailoring education to the needs of the learner. A lifetime educator is a lifetime learner, exploring frameworks about how to think about teaching and learning and various pedagogical approaches to continuously improve their craft. Rather than be overwhelmed by the variety of possible choices, we suggest educators pick a single new construct and a new pedagogy and advance one tool at a time.

6

LEADERSHIP FOR A CURRICULAR APPROACH

"While you perform knowledge work, you learn. And you learn minute by minute if you are to perform knowledge work effectively" (Marquardt, 2011, p. 13). In previous chapters, we explored how the curricular approach is a paradigm shift, how to identify learning aims grounded in the institutional context, and how to design strategies that utilize intentional and diverse pedagogy. This chapter is dedicated to describing ways of leading to best support the design and implementation of a curricular approach. Bennis (1997) says,

> To survive in the 21st century, we're going to need a new generation of leaders—*leaders*, not managers. The distinction is an important one. Leaders conquer the context—the volatile, turbulent, ambiguous surroundings that sometimes seem to conspire against us and will surely suffocate us if we let them—while managers surrender to it. (p. 63)

You cannot manage a curricular approach; you must lead it.

Specifically, in this chapter, we discuss the importance of leading as a learner, leading effective cultural and organizational change, mindful leadership, and leadership strategies consistent with fostering student success and learning. Leadership, in this context, is intended to capture the human capital that is essential for the buy-in, sustainability, and overall impact of the curricular approach.

Leaders as Learners and Educators

Shifting to a curricular approach is a shift from an old way of *doing student affairs work* to a whole new way of *being a student affairs educator*. This means new ways of being, not only individually but also organizationally. It means systematically structuring and sequencing learning initiatives beyond functional silos to align with how students experience college. To successfully lead a curricular approach, individual leaders need to shift to not only a new mind-set but also an entire organizational structures and practices need to shift to being both learner focused and educationally driven. These shifts provide context for the staff, individually and collectively, to work together toward a common purpose (Sinek, 2009). In their book *Learning as a Way of Leading*, Preskill and Brookfield (2009) describe the often overlooked role of learning in leading. The following sections offer perspective on how a continuous commitment to learning, as a key aspect of leading, undergirds the leadership competencies and capabilities required for those committed to the curricular approach.

Create a Learning Organization

Fostering an organizational culture of learning aligns with the focus of providing learning-enhancing environments for students. Much like the importance of being open to learning from assessment to improve educational strategies, student affairs educators in a curricular approach also need to create vibrant learning organizations more generally (Senge, 2006). Marquardt (2011) defined a *learning organization* as "a company that learns effectively and collectively and continually transforms itself for better management and use of knowledge; empowers people within and outside the organization to learn as they work; utilizes technology to maximize learning and production" (p. 247).

Creating communities of learners among professional and student staff and student leaders is critical to expanding our capabilities in ways many student affairs practitioners are not currently comfortable or familiar with. In the authors' experience, working with many different campuses, this often elusive culture shift has been one of the most critical in making a sucessful and sustainable shift to a curricular approach. Choosing to engage more directly with student learning and placing measures of learning more directly into success definitions requires moving out of the familiar for many in student affairs. Some student learning assessment may lead to conclusions that are directly counter to some of the traditional beliefs about what students are gaining beyond the classroom. For instance, student activities staff may find that student organization officers learn more about conflict avoidance than effective conflict management skills.

A leader of a learning organization can teach an organization to celebrate findings of ineffectiveness, incomplete conceptual frameworks, and failed initiatives because of the learning that can result from all of these experiences. Leaders of learning organizations can also promote team learning in direct ways by introducing new models for student learning as part of the normal everyday cycle of work. Leaders can also promote more organic models such as developing opportunities to bravely (Arao & Clemens, 2013) share unit successes and failures; peers presenting their knowledge and new discoveries; or dedicating portions of standing meeting times to educational videos, podcasts, common reads, or mini presentations from conferences related to student learning.

Leading a learning organization may also mean connecting to others on campus you do not know, taking advantage of learning opportunities beyond campus, or working to establish communities of learners beyond your institution or higher education. For example, an office of multicultural life might partner with faculty members with expertise in intergroup dialogue as a pedagogy. Or a staff team in orientation might engage in a common read on the scholarship of the importance of and how to foster a sense of belonging. Educators can also engage students as learning partners (Baxter Magolda & King, 2004), sharing and discussing with them the data from assessment and inviting them to help improve educational strategies.

Foster a Culture of Continuous Improvement

A management mind-set compels us to constantly improve a system or process in a manner where operations run efficiently and effectively with the least amount of physical and psychological energy possible. This approach is admirable, but those leading from a curricular approach to student learning beyond the classroom must accept the following:

- Teaching and learning approaches, especially critical and inclusive practices, can never be perfected (Tuitt et al., 2016). Approaches are based on our *best* understanding of our learners, pedagogy, and ourselves at a particular moment, and as our understanding evolves, so must our practices.
- Facilitating learning is rarely a highly efficient practice. Each step often requires significant amounts of time, brainpower, and emotion.
- A checklist risk is hidden in efficiency models of teaching. Although checklist models can help guide engagement in learning environments,

when educational strategies become routine and highly systemized there is a strong pull toward accomplishing a task and losing the heart of the learning.
- Every new staff member will require a significant skill, knowledge, and habit of mind investment. Each institution pursues an individualized curricular approach and new staff will not arrive ready to immediately help advance the model, though their fresh perspective may instigate creativity, innovation, and new contributions.

In the student affairs arena, it is still wise to have exceptional management approaches so that the essential elements of the operation less related to student learning can be handled with the minimum amount of energy for the heavy investments to be focused on continuous improvement of student learning.

The dynamic nature of the curricular approach means leaders must be prepared to accommodate organizational changes and shifts in campus partnerships, institutional priorities, and the broader societal context beyond campus. Leaders of a curricular approach must be constantly curious (Kashdan, 2010) and less eager to show that they know things and more eager to learn (Dweck, 2008). This cycle of continuous improvement helps foster a culture of positive restlessness (Hatfield & Wise, 2015; Kuh et al., 2010). Positive restlessness is recognizing what is working well and always seeking to improve (Schuh, 2013). In the authors' experience, positive restlessness is about striking that delicate balance between being overly self-critical and being complacent. In a curricular approach, there is always something to learn from a cycle of continuous improvement, from the literature surrounding the identified learning goals and outcomes, on the pedagogy of learning, and new ideas beyond our field. Committing to continuous improvement as a positive aspect of curricular leadership is a healthy way to encounter, interpret, and move forward from real and perceived failures in our work.

Reconsider Professional Development for Scholar Practitioners

Leading curricular approaches is not just about student learning; it is about the learning of leaders, educators, and critically conscious professionals too. Staff members cannot help students learn what they will not explore themselves. Being a learning organization means learning about curricular approaches, learning about the specific content articulated in the goals and outcomes, learning about pedagogy and educational strategies, and learning about the assessment of student learning. Appendix M provides a list of recommended resources as a starting place.

Leadership for a curricular approach means fully embracing student affairs educators as active and engaged scholar-practitioners who are knowledgeable about the research, theory, and practice, both within student affairs and beyond. It also means being scholar-practitioners around the content of the learning (the learning goals and outcomes) and pedagogy (educational strategies). If staff members are focusing on developing resilience to challenging situations with students, how are staff members engaging in that learning themselves? Staff members cannot ask students to engage in dialogues across differences if they are not engaging in those same dialogues themselves. This engagement as learners helps student affairs educators with their praxis (Freire, 1972/2000) and forces them to critically reflect. This ongoing critical reflection becomes an essential assessment tool to improve the design and implementation of educational strategies. Being learning centered means engaging deeply with the content of the educational priority and identified learning goals. As eighteenth-century French philosopher Joseph Joubert (1899) wrote, "To teach is to learn twice over."

Evolutions in professional development, moving beyond the old model of simply conference attendance, and exploring a wide range of methods and content are necessary. As educators develop a curriculum- and syllabus-style approach to student learning beyond the classroom, so too should they create a similar structure within student affairs divisions and departments. What skills, knowledge, and habits of mind do student affairs educators need to be highly effective with their educational priority and related learning goals? What do the current staff members possess now? The gap between these two questions begins to focus the leader on a path to narrow the gap. Full-year team/group learning plans can then be developed. Individual development plans can be created based on the needs of each person and position. Conference attendance moves from random exploration to targeted exploration, with attendees focused on obtaining areas of knowledge to bring back to the department. Highly focused team readings are developed. Individuals demonstrating promise in key areas of the curriculum can be sent to focused workshops and conferences on topics such as assessment and diversity education and return to teach others.

Working to narrow the gap at the organizational level and developing a learning plan for the unit also expands the vision of the leader and offers guidance about the expertise that needs to be brought into the team, through both hiring and campus collaborations. It may mean working with the campus's center for teaching and learning to connect their expertise to the unit. It may mean bringing in experts from the K–12 sector. It might include online modules or group experiences designed to expand creativity such as a visit to a children's museum or a ropes course. When the leader can clearly identify the learning needs for the unit, many successful pathways open to develop the unit as a team of educators.

Learn Beyond Student Affairs and Higher Education

Student affairs educators can learn much from K–12 practices, theory, and educational psychology about how to structure and design learning opportunities. Educators who work beyond the classroom can also learn a great deal from behavioral economics and the research around behavior change and developing new patterns (Heath & Heath, 2007, 2010; Pink, 2009; Thaler & Sunstein, 2009). There is also exciting new understanding about how the brain works and the neuroscience of learning and development (Bresciani Ludvik, 2016; Siegel, 2010). Critical pedagogy (Brookfield, 2005; Freire, 1972/2000; hooks, 1994; Tuitt et al., 2016) helps educators to be more aware of the ways they may be reinforcing dominant and oppressive ways of knowing, teaching, and learning and the liberatory ways of fostering learning.

There is much to be learned from business and those who work for non-profits as well. Many of those organizations have been exploring how to best develop mission-driven cultures, develop human resource talent, and develop ways to maximize the end-user experience. Creative leaders understand how to capture lessons from any context and see the applicability for their own arena. Leadership for the curricular approach involves thinking critically about a vast offering of ideas and resources to consider ways in which priorities, environments, and practices must adapt and evolve to maximize focus on student outcomes.

Leading Organizational Culture and Change

Shifting from a traditional educational approach beyond the classroom to a curricular approach is a major organizational transformation. A general understanding of organizational culture can be particularly helpful when introducing the curricular approach as an organizational change in student affairs. It is important to build on knowledge about organizational culture to consider the art of navigating organizational change through the lens of the curricular approach.

Organizational Change

Change must be well managed throughout the organization as the shift to a curricular approach is made and sustained (Lichterman & Bloom, 2019). Recognizing not all members of the organization will be enthusiastic or even welcoming of such a change can provide a healthy balance between aspiration and reality. Members of the organization and external constituencies will likely experience a wide range of reactions to the decision to make such a shift. Some may initially feel enthusiastic and excited, while others may be apprehensive or afraid. Effective change management means acknowledging a wide range of possible experiences and assisting individuals to work through their different reactions so that each member can best contribute to the new approach. Bridges's (2009) approach recognized the difference between a change event and the transition experience. In this case the change event is a shift to a curricular approach, and the transition includes the individual reactions to this decision and how they evolve over time. Kotter and Cohen's (2002) model recognizes the power of culture and inertia and offers tools to disrupt them and successfully navigate change.

Once a shift to a curricular approach has been made, the change process is ever evolving. Because a curricular approach involves a cycle of continuous improvement, leaders need to be comfortable with change and be able to support others in navigating the ongoing change that comes with a dynamic approach. Examples include annual planning calendars that anticipate the reactive work while carving out time for the essential cycle of review, as well as selection and training processes, which reflect new questions, approaches, and modules so that all employees are thinking about their work in new ways, and this new way of thinking is refreshed and reinforced annually.

Organizational Culture

Successful organizational change requires a shifted organizational culture. Even those leading organizational change and championing a curricular approach can find themselves falling into old patterns and previously ingrained professional practices. Without a cultural change, organizational change is unlikely to be sustained, especially as individuals depart and join the organization. But culture is strong and, much like Newton's first law of physics, will support the status quo unless a powerful force redirects it. This redirection must be intentional and strategic (Collins, 2011; Kuh, 1993). This is especially important in higher education and student affairs work specifically, where staff turnover and change in leadership can result in rapid and frequent institutional change. Creating a culture that is aligned with a student learning focused approach is critical to maintaining this focus among competing and shifting priorities.

Symbolic changes, although small, can be powerful in shifting culture (Bolman & Deal, 2008). The authors have seen innovative and powerful examples of integrating the learning focus into staff T-shirts, brochures, recruitment materials, and images in meeting spaces. All are things that can signal to the organization that this culture has shifted and this shift is here to stay. What leaders say explicitly again and again is also a powerful reminder of what matters. How often have we heard someone reinforce their point by saying, "Remember, the provost is always saying . . ."? These mantras from leadership communicate something powerful throughout the organization. More important still is what leaders do. Appendix L offers a "Divisional Barometer for the Curricular Approach in Student Affairs," which readers can use to begin to assess some of the cultural artifacts related to implementation of and readiness for a curricular approach.

Culture change requires modeling the way, inspiring a shared vision, challenging the process, enabling others to act, and encouraging the heart (Kouzes & Posner, 2007). In an organization moving to a curricular approach, leadership must do what is being asked of all staff (model the way) and ensure that staff know the why behind the what (inspire a shared vision). Leaders need to hire different people and commit to using staff time differently (challenge the process). They need to allow staff to make mistakes and appreciate them as learning opportunities (enable others to act). Leaders need to reward different behavior.

Shifts in what an organization rewards and recognizes, an example of a cultural artifact, can be a significant action that can shift or solidify a culture and is a way to encourage the heart. With a curricular approach, awards and recognitions should be related to achievement of educational aims, development of campus partnerships, assessment successes, or other aspects of the curriculum. Celebrations that are public, versus mail delivery of certificates, for example, reinforce the behavior you want to see throughout the division. What student milestones are celebrated? Celebrating the 250,000 students who entered the fitness center last year is very different from celebrating the 120 students who completed the semester-long healthy eating challenge. With the former, you are affirming mere attendance. With the latter, you are celebrating significant and sustained demonstrated behavior.

Student affairs professionals engaged in the curricular approach benefit from understanding three levels of organizational culture: artifacts, espoused beliefs and values, and basic underlying assumptions (Schein, 2010). First, artifacts are "visible products of the group, such as the architecture of its physical environment; its language; its technology and products; its artistic creations; its style . . . ; its myths and stories told about the organization; its published list of values; and its observable rituals and ceremonies" (p. 23). Within an institution, a division, or a department, there can be hundreds, if not thousands, of examples of artifacts. Leadership for the curricular approach involves recognizing the history, perceptions, meanings, and values associated with such artifacts. Artifacts left unconsidered may contribute to organizational change efforts slowing or failing. Organization charts and structures that have evolved to make managerial practices efficient and effective will likely require changes to build a teaching and learning organization. Position descriptions and approaches to selection, training, appraisal, and promotion built over decades under a different paradigm must also become artifacts that support a new normal. Budgets as organization artifacts must match the new espoused values of the organization. Remaining cognizant of environmental artifacts, regardless of the form in which they appear, is essential for the ongoing efforts described in the previous chapters of this book.

The second level of culture is espoused beliefs and values. Schein (2010) notes there are varying levels with which beliefs and values form in an organization, beginning with an idea and then either progressing into a shared belief or value or not. The social nature of groups is important when considering when espoused beliefs and values live within the fabric of the culture. Leadership for the curricular approach entails an understanding that this level of culture can impact how others within and beyond an organization understand and believe, or disregard, the set of beliefs and values inherent to the curricular work on a given campus. A leader must emphasize approaches that stimulate engagement in student learning throughout the organization where all must be involved and the mere spectators of the process are brought into the process.

Finally, the third level of culture is basic underlying assumptions, or "unconscious, taken-for-granted beliefs and values" (Schein, 2010, p. 24). Schein notes these assumptions have a role in individuals' and groups' behavior, perceptions, thoughts, and feelings. Leadership for the curricular approach can be most impactful when all three levels of organizational culture are considered, explored, and able to be taught to internal and external stakeholders.

Culture change will not be made through one decision, announcement, or a singular change in the ways we do our work. Similarly, culture change will not stick once it has been made unless we continue to reeducate ourselves and reapproach our work. With a culture that embraces learning and curiosity and fosters a culture of positive restlessness, this kind of engagement and learning, relearning, and unlearning can be invigorating, rather than exhausting.

Mindful Leadership

Mindful leadership can help individuals and organizations let go of their individual and collective ego (Holiday, 2016) to focus on students and student learning. Mindfulness is simply the practice of being fully present in this moment, letting go of the past and the future to be fully here (Carroll, 2008), and then being fully present in the next moment. Mindful leadership is grounded in Buddhist perspectives (Suzuki & Dixon, 1970; Whitelaw, 2012), Stoic philosophy (Holiday, 2014), the latest neuroscience and psychological research (Bresciani Ludvik, 2016; Siegel, 2010), and even quantum physics (Wheatley, 1992). Mindful leadership is about being fully present in leadership so that leaders can embrace innovation, creativity, and learning. It means letting go of the need to be an expert and embracing what Suzuki and Dixon (1970) term a *beginner's mind*. They explained, "In the beginner's mind there are many possibilities, in the expert's mind there are few" (p. 21). In this section, the authors explore how mindful leaders find liberation by focusing on what is essential, recognizing what is within their sphere of influence and outside of it, investing in the process not just the product, developing a healthy sense of non-attachment, letting go of needing to be right and of perfectionism, and understanding the place for humor.

Essentialism

Leaders of a curricular approach need to be able to set priorities. Many individuals and organizations are stretched thin because they are trying to be all things to all people. When everything is a priority, nothing is a priority. In his book *Essentialism*, McKeown (2014) describes how to focus on priorities, determine what really matters, and simplify to the most critical goals and action to leverage our influence. He describes the Pareto principle, which states that 80% of our time, energy, and effort results in only 20% of our impact, which means then that conversely only 20% of our time, energy, and effort results in 80% of our impact. If leaders can figure out which time, energy, and effort is having a big impact they can refocus energy on what really makes a difference and have a greater influence.

One of the real assets of a curricular approach is that it helps provide focus and a basis upon which leaders and organizations can decide what is a priority, what is less of a priority, and what is not a priority. When there are clarified goals for student learning it is much easier to identify what actions and initiatives show the most promise and have the biggest return on investment based on assessment of student learning. A curricular approach also aligns implementation with design and strategies with goals and outcomes. This alignment helps streamline efforts and simplify what divisions, departments, and individuals are doing so that they can be more for students.

As individuals and organizations, how can student affairs educators do less so that they can be more? How do they recognize when goals and outcomes are redundant with what other units and other divisions on campus are better positioned to do? How do they recognize when educational strategies are integrated and reinforce each other in ways that foster and support learning or when they are redundant and not a good use of resources? What processes, initiatives, or values would the organization benefit from sunsetting or putting on the list for strategic abandonment? In work with various campuses, the authors have seen teams develop lists of individual and organizational processes that can be considered for elimination to significantly reduce time, energy, and effort. These lists include some items that can be let go immediately and others that become items for strategic abandonment over time.

Sphere of Influence

Many leaders who embrace a more traditional, hierarchical, or industrial approach to leadership feel that they must maintain full control over the organization, people, and even circumstances (Rost, 1991). Mindful leaders recognize that trying to control what is out of their control and beyond their sphere of influence is wasted energy, does not work, and can be incredibly frustrating. In the realm of sports, mindful leaders recognize that outcomes of races and competitions are often out of their control. Coaches cannot control the weather, the officials, or the opponents. Instead, mindful athletic competitors, both coaches and participants, focus entirely on their process. Focusing on the process in this setting means training; practicing; maintaining routines; sleeping; eating; and more broadly harnessing their time, energy, and resources. The more leaders give up trying to control what is beyond their control and simultaneously claim agency for what is within their control, the more effective they can be as leaders.

In a curricular approach, this means not trying to control external circumstances or not waiting until the perfect circumstances exist. Instead, a mindful leader engages with their current circumstances. For example, rather than wait for a new president to start or for a new strategic plan, develop a focus for the curriculum that aligns with the current institutional priorities and adjust as needed. Rather than hold off on implementing a curriculum until all first-year students live in traditional residence halls where they are easier to reach rather than in suites and apartments, embrace the different facilities and design educational strategies specifically for these environments. It might be ideal to have a three-credit course to prepare the health and wellness peer educators for their role; however, the budget or institution's shared governance model might not make that immediately feasible. Instead, embrace the training opportunities that exist and use the coming year as an opportunity to secure resources for such an experience.

Focus on Process

Mindful leaders invest in the process, recognizing that this is necessary to achieve desired results. In a curricular approach, this means not focusing on only one specific endpoint such as a 6% increase in retention between the first year and second year. Instead, a mindful leader attends to processes that are within their influence and that contribute to persistence and retention. These processes might include analyzing the data on student attrition; identifying and engaging with students identified to be at risk for leaving the institution; promoting strategies for overall student well-being and success; and creating broad messaging, communities, and relationships that foster a sense of belonging. By focusing on the processes, we devote our energies within our sphere of influence to more effectively contribute to the institution's goal to increase student persistence and retention.

Healthy Nonattachment

Many of us care so much about our jobs, our roles, and the students we work with that we get in the way of our success and student learning. Mindful leaders choose a middle path or practice healthy nonattachment. Consider a young child holding a frog that has just been caught. The curious child wants to learn about the frog. On one hand, if the child does not hold on, the frog will hop away and an opportunity to learn about the frog can be missed. On the other hand, if the child holds on too tightly to prevent the frog from escaping, the frog can be crushed. The middle path, for the curious child, is to hold the frog gently so that it can be studied without harming the frog and then be released when the child and the frog are ready.

How many times have student affairs educators engaged with a student and determined that, no matter what, this student will pass the class, graduate, not have another conduct violation, or get the internship they desire and deserve? However, sometimes educators are so determined the student will achieve the outcome they have determined for them that they hold on too tightly. Even if they are successful in getting the student to the milestone, which feels good to the staff member, the student has not learned to navigate the challenging situation themselves. Rather, they have learned that staff will help them succeed, which is enabling. Instead, by practicing healthy nonattachment educators can see where the student needs additional support and where the student needs to take responsibility for navigating the challenges before them (which can vary from student to student). When educators choose healthy nonattachment, and support students in learning to navigate complex internal processes and external systems themselves, the staff member will likely not receive nearly as much credit, which mindful leaders do not need, because the student feels that they have navigated the challenge on their own. Student affairs educators need to ensure that they are doing their own healing work through relationships, social support, counseling, coaching, and other means so that staff members do not use students to meet their own unmet emotional needs.

Letting Go

Many student affairs educators who now embrace a curricular approach recognized early on that neither they nor their staff had the educational expertise to facilitate the desired learning content and pedagogy. Leaders must be willing to be transparent about the complexities of facilitating learning, managing their own learning, and assessing learning. This requires letting go of always being right. This letting go does not undermine leadership; it enhances it. When leaders share vulnerability, they build trust (B. Brown, 2018). The continuous improvement cycle of a curricular approach means embracing failure as a learning opportunity. When leaders stop defending initiatives, ideas, and hard work, it is far easier to begin to see what can be done to better foster student learning. Some of the best ideas shared in a conference room do not work in implementation. Some of the ideas that seem just terrible in a conference room in January have turned out to be some of the best ways to foster student learning in dining halls in November. In cultures of fear and scarcity mind-set, innovation and creativity do not happen (B. Brown, 2018). When leaders create cultures in which staff members are not defensive and afraid of failing, but instead are curious and eager to find out what can be modified and improved, learning and growth occur throughout the organization.

At the 2012 ACPA Residential Curriculum Institute, Charles Schroeder, former two-time president of ACPA and Lifetime Achievement award recipient and one of the lead authors of the *Student Learning Imperative* (ACPA, 1996), challenged the perfectionism of many attendees by suggesting that they launch their curricular work at 40%. He shared from his experience that as soon as you launch an effort, you learn so many lessons immediately that you change much right away. If that is the case, why wait three years to implement a curricular approach if you have a year of curricular initiatives mapped out and proofread and assessment strategies ready to go? Instead, let go of perfectionism: Launch at 40%, learn those immediate lessons, adjust for later in the fall semester, and then modify assessment strategies for adjustments made. The authors have found that it can be a jarring shift in perspective for those new to a curricular approach. Schroeder's encouragement to launch at 40% often becomes a long-lasting nudge to avoid perfection and innovate, experiment, take risks, learn, and improve along the way.

In talking about some of the most critical challenges facing modern society, Jon Kabat-Zinn, developer of mindfulness-based stress reduction (MBSR), has said, "This is far too serious a matter to take too seriously" (Tippett & Kabat-Zinn, 2012, para. 166). Letting go of being too serious about the work allows humor to foster creativity, helps us see new solutions, and opens us up to new possibilities. Leaders can use humor to broaden the perspectives of themselves and their organization to tackle very serious challenges more effectively. In a curricular approach, this means leaders take student learning very seriously but they do not take themselves too seriously. This means being open to what they do not know and being willing to laugh at themselves for not knowing. It means being willing to take a risk and try an unusual or innovative initiative with hopefulness but also being curious to know what works and what doesn't. It means being open to engaging unusual partners, realms of knowing, and sources of insight to develop something new, rather than just using the so-called best practice.

Leadership Strategies

A curricular approach organizes student affairs educators' work around student learning. As the authors have seen firsthand, the learning that is aspired to and how that learning is facilitated varies from campus to campus. Different strategies will be required depending on goals, pedagogy, culture, students, and institution specifics. The authors offer a few strategies that we have found work often with organizations using a curricular approach. We encourage you to consider these and their applicability or adaptability for your organization.

Reconsider Everything

Shifting to a curricular approach requires willingness to reassess all aspects of the organization to see how they align with the learning goals and outcomes as well as the educational strategies. A curricular approach cannot be an add-on to the core work of operating the career center or wellness program; it must be a new lens through which those organizations now function. The new lens of this approach means reassessing the organizational structure, staffing patterns, resource allocations, meeting structures, job descriptions and performance evaluations, selection and training, and more. The authors often see folks in the midst of making the switch to a curricular approach feeling overwhelmed. While all changes do not all need to occur immediately, they all need to be examined eventually to determine if and how they can better align with the curricular approach. This assessment and evaluation must be done in an ongoing manner so that the organizational mechanisms continue to be aligned with how the curriculum changes and evolves over time.

Paying attention in politically astute ways to the broader context within and beyond the institution to be sure that the division or department curriculum remains aligned is critical. All processes need to be reassessed to see where and how they fit in the new approach. Often, strategic abandonment of past practice or aspects of the culture can be a way to be most aligned with the present priorities.

Identify Learning Opportunities

As processes and procedures are reassessed, individuals throughout the organization need to be clear on where the aims are customer service and where the aims are student learning. If the aims of a process are customer service, then the process should aim to eliminate obstacles and make the experience as smooth and pleasant as possible. For processes where customer service is the aim, satisfaction can be a good measure of success. Even in an organization operating from a curricular approach, there are still many processes where a customer service approach is a good fit.

If the goal is learning, then a customer service approach all of the time (making the student happy all the time and never saying, "No, you can't do that") is antithetical to achieving the aims of learning. If the outcome of a process is learning, then we want that process to provide just the right level of an obstacle for the student. If the obstacle is too high, then the student becomes overwhelmed and shuts down and learning is unlikely. If the obstacle is too small, then the student does not need to take on any new ways of knowing, being, or doing to navigate the obstacle, and learning is unlikely. For learning to occur we want just the right level of challenge and support for that student (Sanford, 1967). When learning is our goal, satisfaction is rarely a good indicator of success. A student may learn most from a process that they find very unsatisfactory.

Engage Across the Organization

The authors have observed that using and developing the strengths of different team members is a helpful approach in fostering this ongoing process of continuous improvement. We all bring different strengths to our work, whether those be our top five Gallup strengths (Clifton & Anderson, 2001; Rath, 2007) or just those things we have always felt and been told we are particularly good at in our work. In a traditional model, an individual in an organization might need a little bit of everything, determining all the goals and designing all the strategies. In a curricular approach, a leader can create small teams to take on specific aspects of the curriculum and utilize the individual strengths collectively within teams to develop quality learning opportunities that can be applied widely.

Within departments, small teams working independently and sharing their work for feedback and integration with the larger group can help move the overall curriculum forward effectively and efficiently. Across divisions, leaders can rely on the talents of individuals, small teams, and departments to foster networks of learning opportunities for students. If each member of the organization is engaged in the curriculum and giving other members of the organization feedback on their efforts, it improves all aspects of the curriculum, improves ability to give and receive feedback, and fosters better integration of learning initiatives across the student experience and across the organization.

Brain Pickings blog author Maria Popova (2015) has observed, "Critical thinking without hope is cynicism. Hope without critical thinking is naïveté" (para. 2). With a curricular approach, neither cynicism nor naïveté is desired. A curricular approach is not a spectator sport. It requires each member of the organization to engage and be willing to fail, learn, and do better for students each time. This process requires innovation, creativity, and lots of feedback. Some are tempted to avoid the messiness and riskiness of sharing new ideas to contribute to something new, and simply wait to critique the imperfection of others. Those unwilling to take risks will find that their feedback is rarely welcome by those who are taking risks (B. Brown, 2018). They are the cynics. Those who are willing to be messy being innovative and creative find that their feedback is welcome and appreciated. The educators engaged in this way are utilizing hopeful critical thinking.

Align Resources and Planning Processes

The curricular approach helps divisions use resources efficiently and helps staff members to be good stewards of those resources. A budget, not just knowing how much a unit has been allocated for the year, is essential to accomplish and should be an illustration of division and department priorities. If possible, the budget process should align with the curriculum review cycle so that as annual student learning priorities are identified, dollars and human resources can be assigned appropriately. If staff require additional training and professional development, that cost center reflects a commitment to staff development. The cost center for social programs would not exceed a cost center for self-discovery and development initiatives.

The only way everything can change is if a leader plans for the change. Use the division or department strategic planning process to initiate pilots, plan for organizational growth, and change the infrastructure of organizations to better support student learning and success. While the strategic plan may reflect aspirations that do not on the face appear related to your educational aims, it is unlikely that a leader will successfully implement and sustain a curricular approach if all aspects of the organization are not committed to these aims. As the authors have stated previously, everything changes, but it doesn't have to change all at once. Strategic planning allows leaders to lead that change thoughtfully. If it is a well-curated process with an intentional implementation plan (committees with broad and diverse representation, rigorous timeline, and good oversight), the plan can be a powerful force for cultural change and sustained organizational change.

Invest in Learning-Focused Staff Members and Teams

Implementing a curricular approach is an investment in the learning of students. It is also an investment in the staff who are working alongside leadership to develop their skills as educators to best accomplish this work. Investing in this human capital should be strategic and intentional. Stauffer and Kimmel (2019) offered the following recommendations for professional development on the curricular approach and backward design and how to invest in the learning and engagement of housing and residence life staff. The concepts are (a) ensure staff involvement in determining unit learning goals, (b) determine staff competency and knowledge needed to support learning outcomes, (c) develop a guided process with opportunities for practice and feedback, and (d) execute assessment of the approach.

Leaders are most successful when they seek to hire the best employees, those who have a commitment to learning and a growth mind-set and can articulate the value of learning beyond the classroom. Once hired, leaders can support their growth, advocate for advancement when appropriate, and, as the organization evolves to account for the changes resulting from the curricular approach, their voices should be at the table to help guide change. It is impossible to assert that every employee will have a say in every decision or to seek consensus regularly in large and complex organizations. It is possible to recognize the value of incredibly talented employees doing this work and acknowledge that more brains working through a problem are likely to make a better decision than one brain. This is most true when leaders have hired a diverse staff with various experiences, backgrounds, and identities.

Conclusion

Over the past dozen years, a new way of leading has emerged from faculty's and participants' sharing at the ACPA Residential Curriculum Institute and Institute on the Curricular Approach, as well as those working with this approach on individual campuses. This new curricular leadership mind-set was not explicitly articulated or sought, but it is now a very clear and essential aspect to successful implementation of a curricular approach. The ways of leading are not unique to a curricular approach, but they are tied to some of the 10 essential elements, key components of a curriculum, and overall individual and organizational shifts that result with a successful commitment to increased learning for both students and leaders.

Student affairs educators have a long history of individually and collectively working to improve student success. We have evolved as a profession to consider how we can contribute to student learning beyond the classroom. We, the authors of this book, have learned with, from, and among a vast community of learners and leaders on the curricular approach. It has been challenging, illuminating, and invigorating. We look forward to continuing to learn from and with you as this idea, approach, and how we implement it on our campuses evolves. The road is long and the future is bright.

APPENDIX A

Ten Essential Elements for a Curricular Approach

ESSENTIAL ELEMENT 1: The curricular approach is directly connected to institution mission, context, and student populations served.
ESSENTIAL ELEMENT 2: The learning aims including educational priority, learning goals, and learning outcomes are derived from the institutional context.
ESSENTIAL ELEMENT 3: Learning aims and strategies are rooted in scholarship.
ESSENTIAL ELEMENT 4: Learning outcomes drive the development of educational strategies.
ESSENTIAL ELEMENT 5: The curricular approach utilizes a variety of educational strategies to facilitate student learning.
ESSENTIAL ELEMENT 6: Educators who have expertise, in terms of both content and pedagogy, are utilized to design and implement the desired learning.
ESSENTIAL ELEMENT 7: The curricular approach developmentally sequences learning.
ESSENTIAL ELEMENT 8: Campus and community partners are identified and integrated into plans.
ESSENTIAL ELEMENT 9: A curricular approach is developed through a review process.
ESSENTIAL ELEMENT 10: A curricular approach includes a cycle of assessment to improve student learning.

APPENDIX B

Traditional Approaches Versus Curricular Approach to Learning Beyond the Classroom

Traditional	*Curricular*
Identifies list of general topics or categories to which students could be exposed	Clearly defined and more narrowly focused learning aims are tied to institutional mission
Often based on reaction to recent needs displayed by students	Based on scholarly literature, national trends, campus data, and assessment of student educational needs
Student leaders or student staff determine the content within the categories and the pedagogy	Clearly defined learning goals and delivery strategies are written by those with educational expertise
Determining effective pedagogy is often the responsibility of student leaders or student staff members	Lesson plans or facilitation guides developed by educators with necessary expertise provide structure to guide facilitation of educational strategies
Focuses on who will show up to publicized programs	Utilizes a variety of strategies to reach each student
Evaluated based on how many students attend	Assesses student learning outcomes and effectiveness of delivery strategies
Sessions stand alone, disconnected from what has come before or what will come after, and vary by each student leader or staff member	Content and pedagogy are developmentally sequenced to best serve learners
Often in competition with other campus units for students' time and attention	Campus and community partners are integrated into the strategies; content and pedagogy are subject to review (internal and external)

APPENDIX C

Development and Refinement of Educational Aims
Leading to the Development of Educational Plans

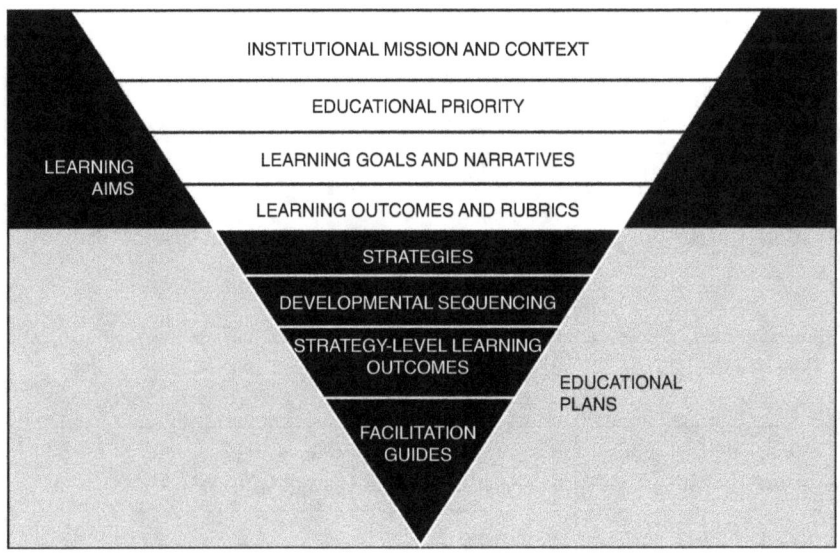

APPENDIX D

Sample List of Artifacts

Institutional strategic plans/blueprints	<ul><li>Mission</li><li>Vision</li><li>Core functions</li><li>Goals</li><li>Aspirations</li></ul>
Division strategic plans/blueprints	<ul><li>Mission</li><li>Vision</li><li>Core functions</li><li>Goals</li><li>Aspirations</li></ul>
General education requirements	<ul><li>Learning objectives</li><li>Requirements</li></ul>
Campus climate study results	<ul><li>Quantitative and qualitative data</li><li>Statements on diversity and inclusion</li></ul>
Assessment data	<ul><li>Division</li><li>Student culture</li></ul>
Repository of campus websites	<ul><li>Institutional leadership: text of speeches and public statements</li><li>Signature learning beyond the classroom programs (i.e., integrative learning)</li><li>Messaging for campus forums</li><li>Organizational charts</li><li>Digital publications including campus newspaper</li></ul>

APPENDIX E

Examples of Learning Aims

Educational Priority

The educational priority articulates the aspirations of what students will take away as a result of their overall educational experience. See the following examples:

- As a result of the student experience at Example University, students will be able to foster a sense of belonging for themselves and others.
- As a result of learning beyond the classroom, students at Sample College will be engaged global citizens.
- As a result of the college experience at Hypothetical University, students will be leaders for the betterment of all.
- As a result of the student experience at Example University, students will contribute to thriving communities.
- As a result of learning beyond the classroom, students at Sample College will foster more equitable communities for all.
- As a result of the college experience at Hypothetical University, students will be engaged citizens fostering sustainable communities.

Learning Goals

Learning goals break down the big idea of the educational priority into more manageable concepts. Examples of learning goals might include identity, relationship, community, equity, well-being, practical competence, inclusion, self-awareness, communication, empowerment, cultural competence, global engagement, and so on.

Learning goals are broken down into learning outcomes and described with a narrative. The narrative is often a three- to five-sentence paragraph that explains what the goals mean in that unique campus context. See the following example:

> **Self-Awareness** (Learning goal label)
> *Students will understand how to be self-aware.* (Learning goal sentence) Self-awareness includes one's ability to accurately describe themselves to others in terms of their strengths, values, personality, and social group identities. It also includes an ability to communicate effectively with others (articulating and listening) about a variety of topics. Self-awareness also includes an ability to engage in conflicts in ways that foster understanding, growth, problem-solving, and mutual respect. Finally, self-awareness is not a status that is achieved but an ongoing process of critical self-reflection. (Narrative)

Learning Outcomes

Learning goals are broken down into learning outcomes and described with a narrative. The narrative is often a three- to five-sentence paragraph that explains what the goals mean in that unique campus context. See the following example:

> **Self-Awareness**: *Students will understand how to be self-aware.*
> Learning outcomes
> Each student will be able to:
>
> - Accurately describe themselves to others.
> - Describe how to communicate effectively in relationships.
> - Engage in conflict in a healthy manner.
> - Practice continued self-reflection around their evolving identity.

Rubric A

Rubrics help organize the developmental sequencing of the learning goals and outcomes. See the following example.

Sample Rubric for Learning Goal

Learning outcome (LO)	None	Beginner	Intermediate	Advanced
LO 1 Accurately describe themselves to others	Cannot accurately describe themselves to others	Can accurately describe some aspects of themselves to others	Can accurately describe themselves in most ways to others	Can accurately describe themselves to others including on how they are changing
LO 2 Describe how to communicate effectively in relationships	Cannot communicate effectively in relationships	Can communicate their needs, emotions, and perspectives of others	Can listen empathically to the needs, emotions, and perspectives of others	Can continue to communicate and make adjustments in relationships based on communication
LO 3 Engage in conflict in a healthy manner	Cannot engage in conflict	Can describe ways to engage in conflict in a healthy manner	Can practice engaging in conflict in a healthy manner in some situations	Can engage in conflict in a healthy manner in most situations
LO 4 Practice continued self-reflection around their evolving identity	Cannot describe themselves to others	Can accurately describe themselves to others	Can describe how they have changed and anticipate ways they may change in the future	Can regularly engage in critical self-reflection as part of healthy growth and development

Strategies

Educational strategies are the ways that student learning is achieved. See the following examples:

- Roommate agreement forms and roommate conflict mediation
- Counseling center–generated content for bulletin boards in residence hall and campus center on cultivating self-awareness
- Short videos with content on communication and conflict
- Workshops on communication and conflict for student organization leaders and athletic captains
- Short videos with seniors sharing how they have changed over the college experience

APPENDIX F

Checklist for Assembling an Educational Plan

UNIT NAME: _____

- **Overview of department** (e.g., conduct, career center, or recreation and wellness center)
  - Mission statement
  - Vision statement
  - Diversity and inclusion statement
  - Core functions
- **Division educational priority**
- **Theoretical framework**
- **Division learning goals**
  - Goal narratives
  - Learning outcomes (for the division and/or department)
- **Rubrics**
- **Overview of learners**
- **Strategy descriptions**
  - A brief paragraph describing how strategies such as workshops, intentional conversations, or retreats will help students achieve the learning goals and outcomes.
- **Sequencing chart**
  - Chart showing how the strategies will be sequenced to achieve learning goals and learning outcomes over time, often by month or week depending on the functional area.
- **Chronological listing of strategies**
  - Content from the sequencing map listed chronologically, often in tables by month. Often includes date/time, strategy, specific focus, and specific learning goals/outcomes.
- **Facilitation guides**
  - Clear descriptions of how the learning will be facilitated for each workshop, campus event, or digital media campaign.
- **Assessment plan**

APPENDIX G

Sample Developmental Sequencing Chart

Learning outcome (LO): Sexual violence prevention	August/September	October	February	April
LO 1 Define three actions that are violations of campus sexual misconduct policies.	Orientation: Policies and resources presented and distributed on cards. Floor meeting: Discussion asking for examples of policy violations and resources.			
LO 2 Demonstrate two ways to intervene as a bystander to prevent sexual violence.		First-year seminar: Discuss bystander intervention and name two examples to prevent sexual violence.	Floor meeting: Invite to share two examples of bystander intervention observed or engaged in.	
LO 3 Take action to prevent sexual violence in their community.				Invite to participate in Clothesline Project or Take Back the Night march, or sign the pledge.

APPENDIX H

Example of Mapping Learning Initiatives Across Departments

Learning outcome (LO): Self-discovery		LO 1 Cultivate curiosity through exploration of new ideas and experiences			LO 2 Develop awareness of individual interests, strengths, and values			LO 3 Develop greater understanding of one's personal identity			LO 4 Draw meaningful connections between identity and purpose		
Career services	Individual appointments	I	R	E	I	R	E	I			I	R	E
Career services	Workshops	I			I	R	E	I	R		I	R	E
Multicultural life	Intergroup dialogue	I	R	E		R		I	R	E	I	R	E
Multicultural life	Leadership retreat	I	R	E		R		I	R	E	I	R	E
Orientation	Large sessions	I			I			I			I		
Orientation	Orientation small-group discussions	I	R		I	R			R		I		
Orientation	Intentional conversations	I	R	E	I	R	E		R				

I = introduced, R = reinforced, E = emphasized

APPENDIX I

Facilitation Guide Template

1. Details of the strategy:
   a. Title of strategy:
   b. Facilitator(s):
   c. Date/time:
   d. Location:
2. Learning desired:
   a. Division/department learning outcomes:
   b. Strategy-level learning outcomes:
3. Target audience(s):
4. Needed supplies/materials:
5. Outline for implementation:
   a. Step 1:
   b. Step 2:
   c. Step 3:
6. Assessment plan:

APPENDIX J

Metacognition

Unconscious incompetence	I don't know that I don't know how to tie my shoes.
Conscious incompetence	I don't know how to tie my shoes. Help me?
Conscious competence	I know how to tie my shoes!
Unconscious competence	I tie my shoes every day, and I don't consciously know how I tie my shoes.

APPENDIX K

Some Potential Pedagogical Strategies

1. Backward design
2. Experiential learning
3. Learning partnerships
4. Peer education
5. Active learning
6. Real-world learning
7. Problem-based learning
8. Critical reflection
9. Assessment as pedagogical strategy
10. Utilizing technological tools
11. Intentional learning spaces
12. Innovate your own pedagogical strategies

APPENDIX L
The Divisional Barometer for the Curricular Approach in Student Affairs

Just as a barometer is a tool to gauge weather conditions, the authors created the following resource to help readers reflect on and inform organizational readiness for implementation of the curricular approach at a division level in student affairs. Similar content for adopting a residential curriculum is available in Lichterman (2016). This tool is designed to help individuals and organizations assess conditions using Bolman and Deal's (2014) four frames of organizations.

Using the Tool

The scale is 1–5, with 5 representing excellent conditions. The ratings can help you gauge organizational readiness.

Step 1: Read and reflect on each bullet.
Step 2: Use the scale to rate the availability of the content for each statement.
Step 3: Average the scores within each frame.
Step 4: Discuss each of the statements in individual and group meetings to discuss the context, presence, and future for each topic.

Structural Frame

Examples of artifacts for this frame: documents and records; communication methods and channels, messages; access to information; position descriptions; assessment findings; processes and time frames

Prompt: To what extent are the various conditions available on your campus to support a curricular approach?	Indicate a score between 1 and 5
Leadership is identified within the division for coordination of messaging.	
Institutional records such as a current strategic plan exist.	
There is access to scholarship to inform educational aims.	
The educational priority statement is written.	
Assessment metrics align with institutional priorities.	
Average score for structural frame	

Human Resources Frame

Examples of artifacts for this frame: team accomplishments; staff roles and student leader roles; training and development

Prompt: To what extent are the various conditions available on your campus to support a curricular approach?	Indicate a score between 1 and 5
Education is provided to staff and student leaders on the 10 essential elements.	
Roles of professional staff are clear according to expertise background.	
Roles of student staff/leaders are clear based on experience.	
Evaluations of professional staff are aligned with tenets of the curricular approach.	
Professional staff training includes the pedagogy of student learning.	
Content for staff development is determined by learning goals for students.	
Average score for human resources frame	

Political Frame

Examples of artifacts for this frame: national priorities; campus priorities; departmental priorities; stakeholder input; feedback solicitation; communication strategies

Prompt: To what extent are the various conditions available on your campus to support a curricular approach?	Indicate a score between 1 and 5
Institutional priorities are easily understood to undergird the curricular approach.	
Efforts to engage stakeholders in academic affairs exist.	

Staff representing their respective departments have opportunities for transparent discussion with others in the division.	
Department leaders believe in the curricular approach to student learning beyond the classroom.	
Budgets are aligned with educational aims.	
Access exists to campus experts on teaching and learning.	
Average score for political frame	

Symbolic Frame

Examples of artifacts for this frame: artifacts and messaging; espoused tenets; campus language used for the curricular approach; organizational culture; addressing challenges; celebration

Prompt: To what extent are the various conditions available on your campus to support a curricular approach?	Indicate a score between 1 and 5
There is a shared understanding of the curricular approach in student affairs.	
Assessment findings of the curricular approach are shared with the campus community.	
Marketing tools exist to publicize the educational aims of the curricular approach to incoming students (e.g., educational priority statement or learning goals).	
Marketing tools exist to publicize the educational aims of the curricular approach to returning students.	
Division-wide celebrations exist to recognize the results of the curricular approach.	
Average score for symbolic frame	

References

Bolman, L. G., & Deal, T. E. (2014). *Reframing organizations: Artistry choice and leadership* (6th ed.). Jossey-Bass.

Lichterman, H. L. (2016). *Organizational perspective on implementing the residential curriculum approach: An ethnographic case study* (Doctoral dissertation). https://scholarcommons.sc.edu/cgi/viewcontent.cgi?article=4821&context=etd

APPENDIX M

Recommended Resources

Overview

American College Personnel Association. (1996). The student learning imperative: Implications for student affairs. *Journal of College Student Development, 37*(2), 118–122.

Keeling, R. P. (Ed.). (2004). *Learning reconsidered: A campus-wide focus on the student experience*. National Association of Student Personnel Administrators and American College Personnel Association.

Kerr, K. G., & Tweedy, J. (2006). Beyond seat time and student satisfaction: A curricular approach to residential education. *About Campus, 11*(5), 9–15.

Kerr, K. G., Tweedy, J., Edwards, K. E., & Kimmel, D. (2017). Shifting to curricular approaches to student learning beyond the classroom. *About Campus, 22*(1), 22–31.

Whitt, E. J. (2006). Are all of your educators educating? *About Campus, 10*(6), 2–9.

Learning and Pedagogy

Adams, M., Blumenfeld, W. J., Catalano, D. C., DeJong, K., Hackman, H. W., Hopkins, L. E., Love, B. J., Peters, M. L., Schlasko, D., & Zuniga, X. (2018). *Readings for diversity and social justice* (4th ed.) Routledge.

Ambrose, S. A., Bridges, M. W., DiPietro, M., Lovett, M. C., & Norman, M. K. (2010). *How learning works: Seven research-based principles for smart teaching*. Jossey-Bass.

Bresciani Ludvik, M. J. (2016). *The neuroscience of learning and development: Enhancing creativity, compassion, critical thinking, and peace in higher education*. Stylus.

Brown, P. C., Roediger, H., & McDaniel, M. (2014). *Make it stick: The science of successful learning*. Belknap.

Freire, P. (1972/2000). *Pedagogy of the oppressed* (30th anniversary ed.). Continuum.

hooks, b. (1994). *Teaching to transgress: Education as the practice of freedom*. Routledge.

Lang, J. M. (2016). *Small teaching: Everyday lessons from the science of learning*. Jossey-Bass.

Rendón, L. (2009). *Sentipensate (sensing/thinking) pedagogy: Educating for wholeness, social justice, and liberation*. Stylus.

Tuitt, F., Haynes, C., & Stewart, S. (2016). *Race, equity, and the learning environment: The global relevance of critical and inclusive pedagogies in higher education.* Stylus.

Assessing Student Learning

Angelo, T. A., & Cross, K. P. (1993). *Classroom assessment techniques: A handbook for college teachers* (2nd ed.). Jossey-Bass.

Bingham, R., Bureau, D., & Duncan, A. G. (2015). *Leading assessment for student success: Ten tenets that change culture and practice in student affairs.* Stylus.

Bresciani, M. J., Gardner, M. M., & Hickmott, J. (2009). *Demonstrating student success: A practical guide to outcomes-based assessment of learning and development in student affairs.* Stylus.

Collins, K. M., & Roberts, D. M. (2012). *Learning is not a sprint: Assessing and documenting student leader learning in cocurricular involvement.* National Association of Student Personnel Administrators.

Gardner, K. G. (2016). Creating an assessment culture. In K. Kennedy (Ed.), *Making a difference: Improving residence life assessment practices* (pp. 133–159). ACUHO-I.

Henning, G., & Roberts, D. M. (2016). *Student affairs assessment: Theory to practice.* Stylus.

Leadership for a Curricular Approach

Bridges, W. (2009). *Managing transitions and change: Making the most of change* (3rd ed.). De Capo.

Brown, B. (2018). *Dare to lead: Brave work, tough conversations, whole hearts.* Random House.

Carroll, M. (2008). *The mindful leader: Awakening your natural management skills through mindfulness meditation.* Trumpeter.

McKeown, G. (2014). *Essentialism: The disciplined pursuit of less.* Crown Business.

Senge, P. M. (2006). *The fifth discipline: The art and practice of a learning organization.* Doubleday.

REFERENCES

Achor, S. (2010). *The happiness advantage: The seven principles of positive psychology that fuel success and performance at work.* Broadway Books.

Adams, M., Bell, L. A., Goodman, D., & Joshi, K. Y. (2016). *Teaching for diversity and social justice* (3rd ed.). Routledge.

Adams, M., Blumenfeld, W. J., Catalano, D. C., DeJong, K., Hackman, H. W., Hopkins, L. E., Love, B. J., Peters, M. L., Schlasko, D., & Zuniga, X. (2018). *Readings for diversity and social justice* (4th ed.). Routledge.

Adams, M., & Zuniga, X. (2016). Core concepts for social justice education. In M. Adams, L. A. Bell, D. J. Goodman, & K. Y. Joshi (Eds.), *Teaching for diversity and social justice* (3rd ed., pp. 95–130). Routledge.

Allen, M. J. (2006). *Assessing general education programs.* Anker.

Almanac. (2017). Profile of freshmen at 4-year colleges, fall 2016. *The Chronicle of Higher Education.* https://www.chronicle.com/article/A-Profile-of-Freshmen-at/240775

Ambrose, S. A., Bridges, M. W., DiPietro, M., Lovett, M. C., & Norman, M. K. (2010). *How learning works: Seven research-based principles for smart teaching.* Jossey-Bass.

American College Personnel Association. (1996). The student learning imperative: Implications for student affairs. *Journal of College Student Development, 37*(2), 118–122.

American Council on Education. (1937). The student personnel point of view. In A. L. Rentz (Ed.), *Student affairs: A profession's heritage* (pp. 66–78). University Press of America.

Anderson, L. W., Sosniak, L. A., & Bloom, B. S. (1994). *Bloom's taxonomy: A forty-year retrospective.* University of Chicago Press.

Angelo, T. A., & Cross, K. P. (1993). *Classroom assessment techniques: A handbook for college teachers.* Jossey-Bass.

Arao, B., & Clemens, K. (2013). From safe spaces to brave spaces: A new way to frame dialogue around diversity and social justice. In L. Landreman (Ed.), *The art of effective facilitation: Reflections from social justice educators* (pp. 135–150). Stylus.

Ashlee, K. C. (2017). Utilizing mindfulness and contemplative practices to promote racial identity development for White college students. *Understanding and Dismantling Privilege, 7*(2), 54–65.

Association of American Colleges & Universities. (2008). *College learning for the new global century.*

Banaji, M. R., & Greenwald, A. G. (2013). *Blindspot: Hidden biases of good people.* Delacorte.

Banta, T. W., Jones, E. A., & Black, K. E. (2009). *Designing effective assessment: Principles and profiles of good practice.* Jossey-Bass.

Barbezat, D., & Bush, M. (2014). *Contemplative practices in higher education: Powerful methods to transform teaching and learning.* Jossey-Bass.

Barkley, E. F., & Major, C. H. (2016). *Learning assessment techniques: A handbook for college faculty.* Jossey-Bass.

Barr, M. J., McClellan, G. S., & Sandeen, A. (2014). *Making change happen in student affairs: Challenges and strategies for professionals.* Jossey-Bass.

Barr, R. B., & Tagg, J. (1995). From teaching to learning: A new paradigm for undergraduate education. *Change, 27*(6), 13–25.

Baxter Magolda, M. B. (2001). *Making their own way: Narratives for transforming higher education to promote self-development.* Stylus.

Baxter Magolda, M., & King, P. M. (2004). *Learning partnerships: Theories and models of practice to educate for self-authorship.* Stylus.

Bell, D. (1992). *Faces at the bottom of the well: The permanence of racism.* Basic Books.

Bennis, W. (1997). *Managing people is like herding cats.* Executive Excellence.

Berila, B. (2016). *Integrating mindfulness into anti-oppression pedagogy: Social justice in higher education.* Routledge.

Berrett, D. (2016, October 16). The next great hope for measuring learning. *The Chronicle of Higher Education.* https://www.chronicle.com/article/The-Next-Great-Hope-for/238075

Bill and Melinda Gates Foundation. (2018). *Today's college students.* https://postsecondary.gatesfoundation.org/what-were-learning/todays-college-students/

Bingham, R., Bureau, D., & Duncan, A. G. (2015). *Leading assessment for studentsuccess: Ten tenets that change culture and practice in student affairs.* Stylus.

Blimling, G. S. (2001). Uniting scholarship and communities of practice in student affairs. *Journal of College Student Development, 42*(4), 381–396.

Blimling, G. S. (2015). *Student learning in college residence halls: What works, what doesn't, and why.* Jossey-Bass.

Block, P. (2008). *Community: The structure of belonging.* Berrett-Koehler.

Bloom, B. S. (1956). *Taxonomy of educational objectives: The classification of educational goals.* Longmans, Green.

Bolman, L. G., & Deal, T. E. (2014). *Reframing organizations: Artistry choice and leadership* (6th ed.). Jossey-Bass.

Bolman, L. G., & Deal, T. E. (2008). *Reframing organizations: Artistry, choice, and leadership* (4th ed.). Jossey-Bass.

Bresciani Ludvik, M. J. (2016). *The neuroscience of learning and development: Enhancing creativity, compassion, critical thinking, and peace in higher education.* Stylus.

Bresciani, M. J., Gardner, M. M., & Hickmott, J. (2009). *Demonstrating student success in student affairs.* Stylus.

Bridges, W. (2009). *Managing transitions: Making the most of change* (3rd ed.). Da Capo Press.

Brookfield, S. D. (2000). Transformative learning as ideological critique. In J. Mezirow (Ed.), *Learning as transformation: Critical perspectives on a theory in progress* (pp. 103–124). Jossey-Bass.

Brookfield, S. D. (2005). *The power of critical theory: Liberating adult learning and teaching.* Jossey Bass.

Brown, B. (2018). *Dare to lead: Brave work, tough conversations, whole hearts.* Random House.

Brown, P. C., Roediger, H., & McDaniel, M. (2014). *Make it stick: The science of successful learning.* Belknap.

Brown, P. G. (2017, March 7). *Does your residential curriculum cascade?* https://paulgordonbrown.com/2017/03/07/does-your-residential-curriculum-cascade/

Brown, R. D. (1972). *Tomorrow's higher education: A return to the academy.* American Personnel and Guidance Association.

Carlson, S. (2018, August 15). Enough 'do more with less.' It's time for colleges to find actual efficiencies. *The Chronicle of Higher Education.* https://www.chronicle.com/article/Enough-Do-More-With/244279/

Carroll, M. (2008). *The mindful leader: Awakening your natural management skills through mindfulness meditation.* Trumpeter.

Chavez, A. F., & Longerbeam, S. D. (2016). *Teaching across cultural strengths: A guide to balancing integrated and individuated cultural frameworks in college teaching.* Stylus.

The Chronicle of Higher Education. (2018, December 31). *Tuition and fees, 1998–99 through 2018–2019.* https://www.chronicle.com/interactives/tuition-and-fees

Clifton, D. O., & Anderson, E. (2001). *StrengthsQuest: Discover and develop your strengths in academics, career, and beyond.* Gallup.

Collins, J. (2011). *Good to great: Why some companies make the leap . . . and others don't.* HarperCollins.

Collins, K. M., & Roberts, D. M. (2012). *Learning is not a sprint: Assessing and documenting student leader learning in cocurricular involvement.* National Associationof Student Personnel Administrators.

Council for the Advancement of Standards in Higher Education. (2019). *CAS professional standards for higher education* (10th ed.).

Davis, T., & Harrison, L. M. (2013). *Advancing social justice: Tools, pedagogies, and strategies to transform your campus.* Jossey-Bass.

Delgado, R., & Stefancic, J. (2017). *Critical race theory: An introduction* (3rd ed.). New York University Press.

Doyle, T., & Zakrajsek, T. (2018). *The new science of learning: How to learn in harmony with your brain* (2nd ed.). Stylus.

Dutch, B., Groh, S., & Allen, D. (2001). *The power of problem-based learning.* Stylus.

Dweck, C. S. (2008). *Mindset: The new psychology of success.* Ballantine Books.

Edwards, K. E. (2006). Aspiring social justice ally identity development. *NASPA Journal, 43*(4), 39–60.

Edwards, K. E., & Gardner, K. (2019, October). Curricular approach: Why, what, and how? Opening plenary presented at the ACPA Institute on the Curricular Approach, Anaheim, CA.

Emdin, C. (2016). *For White folks who teach in the hood—and the rest of y'all too: Reality pedagogy and urban education.* Beacon Press.

Espinosa, L. L., Turck, J. M., Taylor, M., & Chessman, H. M. (2019). *Race and ethnicity in higher education: A status report.* American Council on Education. https://www.equityinhighered.org/resources/report-downloads/

Evans, N. J., Forney, D. S., Guido, F. M., Patton, L. D., & Renn, K. A. (2010). *Student development in college: Theory, research, and practice* (2nd ed.). Jossey-Bass.

Fallucca, A. (2018). *Student Affairs assessment, strategic planning, and accreditation* (New Directions for Institutional Research, No. 175, pp. 89–102.). Jossey-Bass.

Fink, L. D. (2013). *Creating significant learning experiences: An integrated approach to designing college courses (revised and updated).* Jossey-Bass.

Fredrickson, B. (2012). *Positivity: Groundbreaking research reveals how to embrace the hidden strength of positive emotions, overcome negativity, and thrive.* MJF Books.

Freire, P. (1972/2000). *Pedagogy of the oppressed* (30th anniversary ed.). Continuum.

Fried, J. (2016). *Of education, fishbowls, and rabbit holes: Rethinking teaching and liberal education for an interconnected world.* Stylus.

Gardner, K. G. (2016). Creating an assessment culture. In K. Kennedy (Ed.), *Making a difference: Improving residence life assessment practices* (pp. 133–159). ACUHO-I.

Giroux, H. A. (2011). *On critical pedagogy.* Continuum.

Harper, S. R., & Quaye, S. J. (2009a). Beyond sameness, with engagement and outcomes for all: An introduction. In S. R. Harper & S. J. Quaye (Eds.), *Student engagement in higher education: Theoretical perspectives and practical approaches for diverse populations* (pp. 1–16). Routledge.

Harper, S. R., & Quaye, S. J. (2009b). *Student engagement in higher education: Theoretical perspectives and practical approaches for diverse populations.* Routledge.

Harro, B. (2000). The cycle of socialization. In M. Adams, W. J. Blumenfeld, R. Castañeda, H. W. Hackman, M. L. Peters, & X. Zúñiga (Eds.), *Readings for diversity and social justice: An anthology on racism, antisemitism, sexism, heterosexism, ableism and classism* (pp. 15–21). Routledge.

Hatfield, L. J., & Wise, V. L. (2015). *A guide to becoming a scholarly practitioner in student affairs.* Stylus.

Heath, C., & Heath, D. (2007). *Made to stick: Why some ideas survive and others die.* Random House.

Heath, C., & Heath, D. (2010). *Switch: How to change things when change is hard.* Broadway Books.

Henning, G., & Roberts, D. M. (2016). *Student affairs assessment: Theory to practice.* Stylus.

Herrington, A., & Herrington, J. (2006). *Authentic learning environments in higher education.* Information Science Pub.

Hill, M. L. (2009). *Beats, rhymes, and classroom life: Hip-hop pedagogy and the politics of identity.* Teachers College Press.

Holiday, R. (2014). *The obstacle is the way: The timeless art of turning trials into triumph.* Portfolio/Penguin.

Holiday, R. (2016). *Ego is the enemy.* Portfolio/Penguin.

hooks, b. (1994). *Teaching to transgress: Education as the practice of freedom.* Routledge.

Howell, W. C., & Fleishman, E. A. (1982). *Human performance and productivity: Information processing and decision making* (Vol. 2). Erlbaum.

Jensen, E. (2008). *Brain-based learning: The new paradigm of teaching* (2nd ed.). Corwin.

Jones, S. R., & Abes, E. S. (2013). *Identity development of college students: Advancing frameworks for multiple dimensions of identity.* Jossey-Bass.

Joubert, J. (1899). *Joubert: A selection from his thoughts.* Katharine Lyttelton, trans. Dodd, Mead & Co.

Kashdan, T. (2010). *Curious? Discover the missing ingredient to a fulfilling life.* HarperCollins.

Keeling, R. P. (Ed.). (2004). *Learning reconsidered: A campus-wide focus on the student experience.* American College Personnel Association & National Association of Student Personnel Administrators.

Keeling, R. P. (Ed.). (2006). *Learning reconsidered 2: A practical guide to implementing a campus-wide focus on the student experience.* American College Personnel Association, National Association of Student Personnel Administrators, & National Intramural-Recreation Sports Association.

Kegan, R. (2000). What "form" transforms? A constructive-developmental approach to transformative learning. In J. Mezirow (Ed.), *Learning as transformation: Critical perspectives on a theory in progress* (pp. 33–70). Jossey-Bass.

Kennedy, K. (2013). Programming and education. In N. Dunkel & J. Baumann (Eds.), *Campus housing management, residence life and education* (pp. 60–87). Association of College and University Housing Officers, International.

Kerr, K. G., & Tweedy, J. (2006). Beyond seat time and student satisfaction: A curricular approach to residential education. *About Campus, 11*(5), 9–15.

Kerr, K. G., Tweedy, J., Edwards, K. E., & Kimmel, D. (2017). Shifting to curricular approaches to learning beyond the classroom. *About Campus, 22*(1), 22–31.

Kolb, D. A. (1984). *Experiential learning: Experience as the source of learning and development.* Prentice-Hall.

Kotter, J. P., & Cohen, D. S. (2002). *The heart of change: Real-life stories of how people change their organizations.* Harvard Business Review Press.

Kouzes, J. M., & Posner, B. Z. (2007). *The leadership challenge.* Jossey-Bass.

Kuh, G. (2001). College students today: Why we can't leave serendipity to chance. In P. Altbach, P. Gumport, & B. Johnstone (Eds.), *In defense of American higher education* (pp. 277–303). Johns Hopkins University Press.

Kuh, G. D. (1993). *Cultural perspectives in student affairs work.* American College Personnel Association.

Kuh, G. D., Kinzie, J., Schuh, J. H., Whitt, E. J., & Associates. (2010). *Student success in college: Creating conditions that matter.* Jossey-Bass.

Ladson-Billings, G. (1994). *The dreamkeepers*. Jossey-Bass.

Landreman, L., Edwards, K. E., Balón, D. G., & Anderson, G. (2008). Wait! It takes time to develop rich and relevant social justice curriculum. *About Campus*, *13*(4), 2–10.

Lang, J. M. (2016). *Small teaching: Everyday lessons from the science of learning*. Jossey-Bass.

Langer, E. J. (1997). *The power of mindful learning* (2nd ed.). Addison-Wesley.

Lederman, D. (2019, April 17). *Harsh take on assessment . . . from assessment pros*. Inside Higher Education. https://www.insidehighered.com/news/2019/04/17/advocates-student-learning-assessment-say-its-time-different-approach

Lichterman, H. L. (2016). *Organizational perspective on implementing the residential curriculum approach: An ethnographic case study* (Publication No. 101651737, [Doctoral dissertation, University of South Carolina]). ProQuest Dissertations and Theses Global.

Lichterman, H. L., & Bloom, J. L. (2019). The curricular approach to residential education: Lessons for student affairs practice. *College Student Affairs Journal*, *37*(1), 54–67.

Love, B. J. (2000). Developing a liberatory consciousness. In M. Adams, W. J. Blumenfeld, R. Castañeda, H. W. Hackman, M. L. Peters, & X. Zúñiga (Eds.), *Readings for diversity and social justice: An anthology on racism, antisemitism, sexism, heterosexism, ableism, and classism* (pp. 470–474). Routledge.

Love, B. L. (2019). *We want to do more than survive: Abolitionist teaching and the pursuit of educational freedom*. Beacon Press.

Maki, P. L. (2004). Maps and inventories: Anchoring efforts to track student learning. *About Campus*, *9*(4), 2–9.

Marquardt, M. J. (2011). *Building the learning organization: Achieving strategic advantage through a commitment to learning*. Nicholas Brealey.

Marshall, M. S., Gardner, M. M., Hughes, C., & Lowery, U. (2016). Attrition from student affairs: Perspective from those who exited the profession. *Journal of Student Affairs Research and Practice*, *53*(2), 146–159.

Mayhew, M. J., Rockenbach, A. B., Bowman, N. A., Seifert, T. A., Wolniak, G. C., Pascarella, E. T., & Terenzini, P. T. (2016). *How college affects students: 21st century evidence that higher education works* (Vol. 3). Jossey-Bass.

McCormick, A. (2011). It's about time: What to make of reported declines in how much college students study. *Liberal Education*, *97*(1).

McGuire, S. Y., & McGuire, S. (2018). *Teach yourself how to learn: Strategies you can use to ace any course at any level*. Stylus.

McKeown, G. (2014). *Essentialism: The disciplined pursuit of less*. Crown Business.

Medina, J. (2014). *Brain rules (updated and expanded): 12 principles for surviving and thriving at work, home, and school*. Pear Press.

Merriam, S. B., & Bierema, L. L. (2014). *Adult learning: Linking theory and practice*. Jossey-Bass.

Mezirow, J. (2000). *Learning as transformation: Critical perspectives on a theory in progress*. Jossey-Bass.

Nash, R. J., & Jang, J. J. J. (2013). The time has come to create meaning-making centers on college campuses. *About Campus, 18*(4), 2–9.

Nathan, R. (2006). *My freshman year: What a professor learned by becoming a student.* Cornell University Press.

Palmer, P. J. (1998). *The courage to teach: Exploring the inner landscape of a teacher's life.* Jossey-Bass.

Patel, L. (2016). *Decolonizing educational research: From ownership to answerability.* Routledge.

Patton, L. D., Renn, K., Guido, F. M., & Quaye, S. J. (2016). *Student development in college: Theory, research, and practice* (3rd ed.). Jossey-Bass.

Pink, D. H. (2009). *Drive: The surprising truth about what motivates us.* Riverhead.

Popova, M. (2015). Hope, cynicism, and the stories we tell ourselves. *Brain Pickings.* https://www.brainpickings.org/2015/02/09/hope-cynicism/

Preskill, S., & Brookfield, S. (2009). *Learning as a way of leading: Lessons from the struggle for social justice.* Jossey-Bass.

Quaye, S. J., Aho, R. E., Jacob, M. B., Domingue, A. D., Guido, F. M., Lange, A. C., Squire, D., & Stewart, D.-L. (2018). *A bold vision forward: A framework for the strategic imperative for racial justice and decolonization.* College Student Educators International.

Rath, T. (2007). *StrengthsFinder 2.0.* Gallup.

Rath, T., & Harter, J. K. (2010). *Wellbeing: The five essential elements.* Gallup.

Rendón, L. (2009). *Sentipensante (sensing/thinking) pedagogy: Educating for wholeness, social justice, and liberation.* Stylus.

Renn, K. A., & Reason, R. D. (2013). *College students in the United States: Characteristics, experiences, and outcomes.* Jossey-Bass.

Rost, J. C. (1991). *Leadership for the twenty-first century.* Praeger.

Sanders, L. H. (2018). *The influence of residential curriculum on first year residential students in higher education* (Publication No. 10751341, [Doctoral dissertation, University of Alabama]). ProQuest Dissertations and Theses Global.

Sanford, N. (1967). *Where colleges fail: A study of the student as a person.* Jossey-Bass.

Schein, E. H. (2010). *Organizational culture and leadership* (4th ed.). Jossey-Bass.

Schoem, D. L., & Hurtado, S. (2001). *Intergroup dialogue: Deliberative democracy in school, college, community, and workplace.* University of Michigan Press.

Schreiner, L., Louis, M., & Nelson, D. (Eds.). (2012). *Thriving in transitions: A research-based approach to college success.* National Resource Center for the First-Year Experience and Students in Transition.

Schuh, J. H. (2013). *Developing a culture of assessment in student Affairs* (New Directions for Student Services, No. 142, pp. 89–98). Jossey-Bass.

Schwartz, B. (2005). *The paradox of choice: Why more is less.* HarperCollins.

Seemiller, C., & Grace, M. (2019). *Generation Z: A century in the making.* Routledge.

Seligman, M. E. P. (2011). *Flourish: A visionary new understanding of happiness and well-being.* Free Press.

Senge, P. M. (2006). *The fifth discipline: The art and practice of a learning organization.* Doubleday.

Shireman, R. (2016, April 7). *SLO madness*. Inside Higher Education. https://www.insidehighered.com/views/2016/04/07/essay-how-fixation-inane-student-learning-outcomes-fails-ensure-academic-quality

Shushok, F., Arcelus, V., Finger, E., & Kidd, V. (2013). Academic initiatives. In N. Dunkel & J. Baumann (Eds.), *Campus housing management, residence life and education* (pp. 25–59). Association of College and University Housing Officers, International.

Siegel, D. J. (2010). *Mindsight: The new science of personal transformation*. Bantam Books.

Sinek, S. (2009). *Start with why: How great leaders inspire everyone to take action*. Portfolio.

Smith, L. T. (2012). *Decolonizing methodologies: Research and indigenous peoples* (2nd ed.). Zed Books.

Stauffer, C., & Kimmel, D. (2019). A framework for increasing residence life and housing staff capacity and confidence to develop and implement a residential curriculum. *Journal of College and University Student Housing, 45*(3), 24–37.

Sutton, B. Z. (2016, June 20). *Higher education's public purpose*. https://www.aacu.org/leap/liberal-education-nation-blog/higher-educations-public-purpose

Suzuki, S., & Dixon, T. (1970). *Zen mind, beginner's mind*. Walker/Weatherhill.

Thaler, R. H., & Sunstein, C. R. (2009). *Nudge: Improving decisions about health, wealth, and happiness*. Penguin Books.

Tippett, K., & Kabat-Zinn, J. (2012). *Opening to our lives* [Audio podcast]. On Being. https://onbeing.org/programs/jon-kabat-zinn-opening-to-our-lives/

Tuitt, F., Haynes, C., & Stewart, S. (2016). *Race, equity, and the learning environment: The global relevance of critical and inclusive pedagogies in higher education*. Stylus.

Twenge, J. M. (2017). *iGen: Why today's super-connected kids are growing up less rebellious, more tolerant, less happy—and completely unprepared for adulthood and (what this means for the rest of us)*. Atria.

Wheatley, M. J. (1992). *Leadership and the new science: Learning about organization from an orderly universe*. Berrett-Koehler.

Whitelaw, G. (2012). *The Zen leader: 10 ways to go from barely managing to leading fearlessly*. Career Press.

Whitt, E. J. (2006). Are all of your educators educating? *About Campus, 10*(6), 2–9.

Wiggins, G. P., & McTighe, J. (2005). *Understanding by design* (expanded 2nd ed.). Association for Supervision and Curriculum Development.

Willingham, D. T. (2009). *Why don't students like school? A cognitive scientist answers questions about how the mind works and what it means for the classroom*. Jossey-Bass.

Wilson, S. (2008). *Research is ceremony: Indigenous research methods*. Fernwood.

Wyllie, J. (2018, February 13). The 7 things students think about when choosing a college. *The Chronicle of Higher Education*. https://www.chronicle.com/article/The-7-Things-Students-Think/242544

Zadina, J. N. (2014). *Multiple pathways to the student brain: Energizing and enhancing instruction*. Jossey-Bass.

ABOUT THE AUTHORS

Kathleen G. Kerr serves as the associate vice president for student life at the University of Delaware (UD). Kerr provides leadership to enhance the operations, programs, and services for Residence Life and Housing (RLH), the Office of Orientation and Transition Programs, the university student centers, fraternity and sorority leadership and learning, student wellness and health promotion, the Center for Counseling and Student Development, and Student Health Services in a manner that connects the strengths and assets of these units to enhance the campus experience for all students. Kerr is an assistant professor in UD's Department of Human Development and Family Sciences. She has taught several courses at both the master's and doctorate levels and teaches a first-year seminar each semester. She also serves as a permanent member of the Faculty Senate General Education Committee. Kerr was one of the developers of the Residential Curriculum Model and is a founder of the ACPA Residential Curriculum Institute (RCI). She has coauthored several articles about the curriculum model and has served as a faculty member for the RCI and the Institute on the Curricular Approach (ICA). She has consulted with several campuses, helping them to design and develop a curricular approach beyond the classroom. Kerr has been a leader with ACPA College Student Educators International, serving as chair of the Commission for Housing and Residential Life, chair of the Convention Program Team in 2009, and cochair in 2011. She was elected ACPA vice president in 2012, served as president in 2013, and served as past president in 2014. Kerr is the proud recipient of the Indiana University Department of Higher Education and Student Affairs Elizabeth A. Greenleaf Distinguished Alumnus award and was an ACPA Diamond honoree, both in 2010. In 2013 she received an ACPA Annuit Coeptis award as a senior professional. In 2017, Kerr received ACPA's Excellence in Practice award. Kerr attended Indiana University in Bloomington, where she received both her bachelor's in psychology and her master's in college student personnel administration. In 1998 she earned her educational doctorate in educational leadership from UD.

Keith E. Edwards helps individuals, organizations, and communities to realize their fullest potential as a speaker, consultant, and coach. He has spoken and consulted at more than 200 colleges and universities; presented more than 200 programs at national conferences; and written more than 20 articles or book chapters on sexual violence prevention, men's identity, curricular approaches, and social justice education. He has facilitated or cofacilitated two-day workshops on designing and implementing a curricular approach with more than 50 different campuses. He is cohost of *Student Affairs Live* on the Higher Ed Live network. He has received national awards and recognition for his research, writing, and speaking, including an ACPA doctoral writing award, and he was an ACPA Diamond honoree. Edwards coedited the book *Addressing Sexual Violence in Higher Education* (Jossey-Bass, 2018). His TEDx Talk on sexual violence prevention has been viewed around the world. Edwards was the director of campus life at Macalester College in St. Paul, Minnesota, from 2007 to 2015, where he provided leadership and developed a curricular approach for the areas of residential life, student activities, conduct, and orientation. Edwards earned his PhD from the college student personnel administration program at the University of Maryland, where he worked for a living-learning program and completed his dissertation "'Putting My Man Face On': A Grounded Theory of College Men's Gender Identity Development." Edwards earned his MA in the Student Affairs in Higher Education program at Colorado State University and his BA in social studies with a teaching minor and license from Hamline University.

Amanda R. Knerr serves as the executive director of residential life and housing at Indiana State University. She cochaired the ACPA RCI in 2015 and 2016. Knerr served as faculty for the institute from 2010 to 2019. She has consulted with a variety of campuses, developing their curricular approach. Knerr has participated in a variety of ACPA leadership roles including chair of the Commission for Assessment and Evaluation and invited faculty for the ACPA Student Affairs Assessment Institute. In 2017, she was an ACPA Diamond honoree. Knerr received her bachelor's degree in psychology from Wittenberg University, her master's degree in student affairs administration in higher education from Ball State University, and her doctorate in higher education administration from Pennsylvania State University. Knerr's research interests include curriculum development and instructional pedagogy, engaged scholarship, social entrepreneurship, and the development of professional identity.

Hilary L. Lichterman serves as the associate director of residence life at the University of South Carolina. Her dissertation, "Organizational Perspective on Implementing the Residential Curriculum Approach: An Ethnographic Case Study," was the first published research on the curricular approach in student affairs and specifically in housing and residence life. Additionally, Lichterman and J.L. Bloom (2019) authored the article "The Curricular

Approach to Residential Education: Lessons for Student Affairs Practice." Lichterman has presented at numerous local, regional, and national conferences; maintains involvement in ACPA and ACUHO-I; and has conducted on-site consultations and external reviews on the curricular approach in student affairs and housing and residence life with five campuses. She served as the cochair of ACPA's 2013 RCI and as an RCI faculty member from 2014 to 2019. Lichterman earned a bachelor's degree in Spanish and psychology from Marquette University in Milwaukee, Wisconsin; a master's degree in student affairs administration in higher education from Ball State University in Muncie, Indiana; and a doctorate in educational administration in higher education from the University of South Carolina in Columbia. Her professional interests include the curricular approach in student affairs, living and learning communities, organizational culture and change, staff training and development, and emergency preparedness.

James Tweedy is the director of residence life and housing at UD and an adjunct professor within the higher education policy and student affairs program at West Chester University Pennsylvania and focuses his professional energies on exploring the connections between residence life staff inputs into the student experience and the resulting student learning and development gains. Tweedy received his master's in adult and higher education from Montana State University and his educational doctorate in educational leadership from UD. Tweedy has worked in residence life since his first resident adviser job in 1986 and continues to value every minute of the experience. Tweedy is the coauthor of "Beyond Seat Time" and "Satisfaction and Shifting to Curricular Approaches to Learning Beyond the Classroom," published in *About Campus*. Tweedy also codeveloped the first ACPA RCI and continues to serve on the institute faculty regularly.

INDEX

AAC&U. *See* Association of American Colleges & Universities
ABET. *See* Accreditation Board for Engineering and Technology
accountability systems, 85
Accreditation Board for Engineering and Technology (ABET), 26
ACPA. *See* American College Personnel Association
ACPA Institute on the Curricular Approach (ICA), xiv, 21, 113
ACPA Residential Curriculum Institute, 108, 113
active learning, 90
Adams, M., 87
Advancing Social Justice (Davis and Harrison), 86
Allen, M. J., 7
Ambrose, S. A., 81
American College Personnel Association (ACPA), xiii, 5, 21
andragogy, 86
Angelo, T. A., 69
archeological dig, for learning aims
   activities relating to, 42–44
   artifacts included in, 41–42
   core team for, 41–43
   educational aims, development and refinement of, 40–41, 56, 117
   process of, 40–44
   results of, 44
   technological tools used for, 43
   worksheet used for, 43–44
"Are All of Your Educators Educating?" (Whitt), 12
artifacts, 118
   with archeological dig, 41–42
   cultural, 103–4
Assessing General Education Programs (Allen), 7
assessment, 36, 37. *See also* design, implement, and assess
   of learning outcomes, 51
   as pedagogical strategies, 92–93
assessment plans
   benefits of, 68
   comprehensive, 68–69
   cycle of assessment with, 36–37, 69–70
   tools for, 69
Association of American Colleges & Universities (AAC&U), 11, 26

backward design pedagogical strategy, 88
Barbezat, D., 87
Barkley, E. F., 69
Baxter Magolda, Marcia, 3, 32–33
"Beyond Seat Time and Student Satisfaction, xiii
Bloom's taxonomy, 49, 50, 51, 66, 77
brain function, neuroscience and, 78–79
Brain Picking (Popova), 111
Brookfield, S., 97

INDEX

Brown, P. C., 80
Bush, M., 87

campus and community partners identified, 34–35
campus partnerships growth, 16
CAS. *See* Council for the Advancement of Standards in Higher Education
center student learning, 5
chart, developmentally sequenced learning, 61–63, 124
Chavez, A. F., 86
CIRP Freshman Survey, 41
classroom. *See* student learning beyond classroom
Classroom Assessment Techniques (Angelo & Cross), 69
Clothesline Project, 61
cocurricular transcripts, 2
college experience, 55
"College Students Today" (Kuh), 7
Commission for Housing and Residential Life, 21
commitment, continuous improvement culture, 99
communities
  of learners, 97
  of practice, 6
community living, 28
competency, 2, 31–32
comprehensive assessment plans, 68–69
contemplative-based learning practices, 78
contemplative pedagogy, 87
content and pedagogy utilization
  competency relating to, 31–32
  partnership relating to, 32–33
  preparations relating to, 31
continuous improvement
  considerations for, 70–72
  cycle of, 13, 15, 32, 35–36
  with essential elements, 22
continuous improvement culture
  commitment to, 99
  cycle of, 99
  principles of, 98–99
core team, for archeological dig, 41–43
cost of higher education, 2
Council for the Advancement of Standards in Higher Education (CAS), 12, 21, 26, 36
creation, of organizations, 97–98
critical and inclusive pedagogy, 85–86, 101
critical reflection, 92
critical thinking, 111
critique. *See* traditional educational approach critique
Cross, K. P., 69
cultural artifacts, 103–4
culture
  continuous improvement, 98–99
  organizational, 102–4
curricular approach
  context and guidance for, 17
  description of, 3–5, 19–20
  impact of, 14–17
  traditional approach *versus*, 3–4, 20, 116
curricular term, ix, 3
cycle, 69–70
  of assessment, 36–37
  of continuous improvement, 13, 15, 32, 35–36, 99

Davis, T., 86
Degree Qualifications Profile (DQP), 12
design, 23, 31–32

backward, pedagogical strategy, 88
of pedagogy, 12, 58, 59
process, 22
design, implement, and assess, 55
   assessment plans, 68–70
   conclusion to, 72
   continuous improvement with, 70–72
   developmentally sequenced learning, 60–65
   educational plan document, 67–68
   educational plans, 56–57, 67–68, 117, 123
   educational strategies, 23, 28–30, 37, 57–60
   facilitation guides, 28, 65–67, 126
developmentally sequenced learning, 33–34, 66
   chart for, 61–63, 124
   content and pedagogy relating to, 60, 61
   integration and reinforcement with, 60–61, 63
   mapping for, 63–65, 125
   networked approach to, 61
direct approach, for learning process, 82
"Divisional Barometer for the Curricular Approach in Student Affairs," 103
   human resources frame, 130
   political frame, 130–31
   structural frame, 129–30
   symbolic frame, 131
   tools for, 129
division-wide learning outcomes, 48–49, 57
DQP. *See* Degree Qualifications Profile

Dutch, B., 91

educational aims
   development and refinement of, 40–41, 56, 117
   identification of, 7–8
educational needs, of students, 2–3
educational plans, 56–57, 117
   checklist for, 123
   document for, 67–68
educational priority, 24, 28
   development of, 45
   of learning aims, 44–45, 119
   learning goals, learning outcomes, and, 25–26
   themes relating to, 44
educational strategies. *See also* traditional educational approach critique
   checklist for, 58
   development of, 28–29
   learning outcomes impacted by, 58–59
   opportunities for, 57, 59–60
   pedagogy relating to, 58, 59
   for student learning, 23, 28–30, 37
   teams for, 59–60
   utilization of, 29–30
educator philosophy, 6–7
educators, leaders as, 97
employability outcomes, 2
engage across organization, 110–11
engaged pedagogy, 86, 87
engagement, of stakeholders, 35, 36, 44, 54, 130
environment transition, xi
espoused beliefs and values, with organizational culture, 103–4
espoused competency-based education, 2

essential elements, for a curricular approach, 10, 54, 73, 85, 99, 113
   campus and community partners identified, 34–35
   chart of, xv, 23, 115
   content and pedagogy utilization, 31–33
   creation of, xiv
   cycle of assessment to improve student learning, 36–37
   developmentally sequenced learning, 33–34
   educational priority, learning goals, and learning outcomes, 25–26
   educational strategies development, 28–29
   educational strategies utilization, 29–30
   focus on, 17
   as guiding framework, 21
   institution mission, context, and student populations served, 22–24
   learning aims and strategies in scholarship, 27–28
   review process development, 35–36
essentialism
   goals and outcomes relating to, 105–6
   priorities relating to, 105
Essentialism (McKeown), 105
"Essential Learning Outcomes," 11
evolutions
   in scholar-practitioners development, 100
   of student affairs, 5–6
experience, of college, 55

experience value, of learning, 2
experiential learning models, 88
experts, 31–33, 34–35

Facebook Live, 93
facilitation guides
   detail level in, 65
   sequencing relating to, 66
   strategy-level learning outcomes articulated by, 28, 65–66
   template for, 67, 126
focus, 7, 17, 23, 107
   learner-focused approach, 11, 58
   learning-focused language, 15
   learning-focused staff members and teams investment, 112
foundational questions, 13
framework, learning rubrics, 51–52, 55
"From Teaching to Learning," 11

goals. *See also* learning goals; learning goals, narratives of
   with essentialism, 105–6
   lack of strategies and, 8
   shared, 34–35

Harrison, L. M., 86
healthy nonattachment, of leadership, 107–8
HERI. *See* Higher Education Research Institute
higher education
   cost of, 2
   initiatives for, 2, 6
   responsibilities of, 1
   societal expectations of, 2
Higher Education Research Institute (HERI), 33–34
How Learning Works (Ambrose et al.), 81

human resources frame, of
    organizations, 130

ICA. *See* ACPA Institute on the
    Curricular Approach
identification
    of campus and community
        partners, 23, 34–35
    of educational aims, 7–8
    of learning aims, 39, 40–54,
        119–20
identity-affirming, equitable,
    justice-oriented, learning as, 86
identity development, 5
implement, 23, 31–32. *See also*
    design, implement, and assess
improvement. *See* continuous
    improvement; continuous
    improvement culture
informed decisions, of student
    affairs educators, 3
initiatives, for higher education, 2, 6
innovation, of own pedagogical
    strategies, 94–95
Instagram, 93
institutional review boards (IRBs),
    68
institution mission, context, and
    student populations served
    curricular design process with, 22
    educational priority with, 24
    focus with, 23
    intersectionality with, 24
    learning goals and outcomes
        relating to, 23–24
    vision with, 22
integration, developmentally
    sequenced learning, 60–61, 63
intentional learning spaces, 94
intersectionality, 5
    with institution mission, 24
    lack of, 9
interweaving learning process, 80
investment, in learning-focused staff
    members and teams, 112
IRBs. *See* institutional review boards

Jang, J. J. J., 94

Kabat-Zinn, Jon, 109
Keeling, R. P., 3, 5, 6, 11–12, 21
Kerr, Kathleen G., xiv, 74
key educational strategies, 37
King, Patricia M., 3, 32–33
knowledge, learning, and pedagogy
    accountability systems relating
        to, 85
    perspective on, 84–88
    social inequities relating to, 85
    as socially constructed, 84
    systems of power and oppression
        impact on, 84–86
knowledge learning, 77–78
Kuh, G., 7

Lang, J. M., 77
leaders, as learners and educators,
    97
leadership, 96
    conclusion to, 113
    continuous improvement culture
        fostered with, 98–99
    essentialism relating to, 105–6
    healthy nonattachment of, 107–8
    leaders as learners and educators,
        97
    learn beyond student affairs and
        higher eduction, 101
    learning organization creation,
        97–98
    letting go, 108–9
    mindful, 104–5, 107

organizational culture and change led by, 101–4
process focus, 107
professional development, for scholar practitioners, 99–101
sphere of influence, 106–7
leadership strategies
align resources and planning process, 111–12
engage across organization, 110–11
identify learning opportunities, 110
invest in learning-focused staff members and teams, 112
reconsider everything, 109–10
LEAP. *See* Liberal Education and America's Promise
learn beyond student affairs and higher eduction, 101
learner-focused approach, 11, 58
learners, changing populations of, 83–84
learning. *See also* student learning; student learning beyond classroom
cumulative value of, 60–61
description of, 11–12
educational value of, 2
identity-affirming, equitable, justice-oriented, 86
mindful, 78
neuroscience of, 78–79
pedagogy, knowledge, and, 84–88, 100
real-world, 90–91
social justice-oriented, 86, 88
transformative, 78
types of, 77–78
understanding of, 76–77
learning aims, 55
considerations for, 54
educational priority of, 44–45
strategies and, in scholarship, 27–28
with student affairs educators, 39–40
learning aims, identification of, 39
archeological dig relating to, 40–44
conclusion to, 52–54
educational priority, 44–45, 119
learning goals, 45–51, 119–20
learning rubrics, 51–52
Learning as a Way of Leading (Preskill and Brookfield), 97
Learning Assessment Techniques (Barkley & Major), 69
learning-enhancing environments, 97
learning-focused language, 15
learning-focused staff members and teams investment, 112
learning goals, 25–26, 28
development of, 46
examples of, 45
outcomes and, 23–24
understanding of, 46–47
learning goals, narratives of, 49, 51
self-awareness, 47–48, 50, 120
strategies for, 47–48
vetting of, 48
learning models, experiential, 88
learning opportunities
beyond classroom, 1–2
identification of, 110
learning organization creation
communities of learners align with, 97
goals of, 97–98
learning enhancement environments align with, 97

learning outcomes, 24, 25–26
　assessment of, 51
　development of, 23, 28–29, 48–49
　division-wide, 48–49, 57
　educational strategies impact on, 58–59
　self-awareness, 50, 120
　strategies for, 50, 122
　strategy-level, 28, 65–66
Learning Partnerships (Baxter Magolda & King), 3, 32–33
learning partnerships, principles of, 89
learning practices, contemplative-based, 78
learning process
　components of, 80
　direct approaches with, 82
　metacognition relating to, 81, 127
　mind-set with, 82–83
　pedagogy with, 82
　for student issues, 82
learning process effort, 80
Learning Reconsidered (Keeling), 3, 5, 6, 11–12, 21
Learning Reconsidered 2 (Keeling), 5
learning rubrics, 120–21
　framework for, 51–52, 55
　sample of, 52–53
learning spaces, intentional, 94
letting go, 108–9
Liberal Education and America's Promise (LEAP), 39
liberatory pedagogy, 85
Longerbeam, S. D., 86

Major, C. H., 69
Make it Stick (Brown et al.), 80

Maki, P. L., 63
"Map and Inventories: Anchoring Efforts to Track Student Learning" (Maki), 63
mapping, for developmentally sequenced learning, 63–65, 125
massive open online courses (MOOCs), 2
MBSR. *See* mindfulness-based stress reduction
McKeown, G., 105
meaning-making centers, 94
measured success, with paradigm shift, 16–17
metacognition, 81, 127
mindful leadership, 104–5, 107
mindful learning, 78
mindfulness, 78, 79, 87, 105, 109
mindfulness-based stress reduction (MBSR), 109
mind-set, learning process, 82–83
mindsight, 78
mobile technology, 83
models
　experiential learning models, 88
　of organizational culture, 103
MOOCs. *See* massive open online courses
motivation, learning process, 80
My Freshman Year: What a Professor Learned by Becoming a Student (Nathan), 10
myths, of student affairs educators, 75

Nash, R. J., 94
Nathan, Rebekah, 10
National Survey of Student Engagement (NSSE), 10, 16, 33, 41

networked approach, developmentally sequenced learning, 61
neurogenesis, 78
neuroplasticity, 78–79
neuroscience of learning, 87
  brain function relating to, 78–79
  insights into, 79
NSSE. *See* National Survey of Student Engagement

Office of New Student Orientation, 56
oppression impact, 84–86
organizational culture
  artifacts with, 103–4
  basic underlying assumptions, 103, 104
  espoused beliefs and values with, 103–4
  models of, 103
  recognition with, 103
  rewards with, 103
  shifts in, 102–3
organizations
  change in, 101–2
  creation of, 97–98
  engage across, 110–11
  human resources frame of, 130
  political frame of, 130–31
  structural frame of, 129–30
  symbolic frame of, 131
outcomes. *See also* learning outcomes
  employability, 2
  with essentialism, 105–6
  "Essential Learning Outcomes," 11
  transformative education, 12

paradigm shift rationale
  campus partnerships growth with, 16
  continuous improvement with, 15
  curricular approach to, 12
  impact of, 14–17
  measured success with, 16–17
  shared student learning-focused language with, 15
  student learning gains with, 14–15
  teacher-centric to learner-focused, 11, 58
The Paradox of Choice (Schwartz), 10
Pareto principle, 105
partnerships, 3, 16, 32–33, 89
PBL. *See* problem-based learning
pedagogical strategies, 128
  active learning, 90
  assessment as, 92–93
  backward design, 88
  critical reflection, 92
  experiential learning models, 88
  innovation of own, 94–95
  intentional learning spaces, 94
  learning partnerships, 89
  PBL, 91–92
  peer education, 89–90
  real-world learning, 90–91
  technological tool utilization, 93
pedagogy, 13, 16, 28, 29
  approaches to, 84
  contemplative, 87
  content and, xv, 4, 9, 15, 23, 27, 31–33, 60, 61
  critical and inclusive, 85–86, 101
  definition of, 84
  design of, 12, 58, 59

engaged, 86, 87
learning, knowledge and, 84–88, 100
with learning process, 82
liberatory, 85
of the oppressed, 86
student affairs educators relating to, 75–76
peer education, 89–90
peer review, 36
performance-based funding metrics, 2
Pinterest, 93
planning process, 111–12
plans, 34–35, 100
assessment, 23, 36–37, 68–70
educational, 56–57, 67–68, 117, 123
political frame of organizations, 130–31
Poll Everywhere, 43
Popova, Maria, 111
populations of learners, 83–84
The Power of Problem-Based Learning (Dutch et al.), 91
Preskill, S., 97
principles
of continuous improvement culture, 98–99
Pareto principle, 105
priorities. *See also* educational priority
of essentialism, 105
problem-based learning (PBL), 91–92
process
design, 22
focus on, 107
of learning aims, 40–44, 80–83
planning, 111–12
of review, 23, 35–36

professional development, for scholar practitioners, 99–101

Qualtrics, 43

RA. *See* resident advisor
RCI. *See* Residential Curriculum Institute
Readings for Diversity and Social Justice (Adams et al.), 87
real-world learning, 90–91
recognition, with organizational culture, 103
reconsider everything, as leadership strategy, 109–10
reinforcement, with developmentally sequenced learning, 60–61, 63
Rendón, L., 87
residence halls
essential elements of curricular approach relating to, 21
student learning in, 20–21
resident advisor (RA), ix–xii
Residential Curriculum Institute (RCI), xiii, 14, 21
Residential Life, 16
resources
alignment of planning process and, 111–12
human resources frame, of organizations, 130
for student affairs educators, 75–76
rethinking of student affairs educators, 74–76
retrieval with learning process, 80
review process development
peer review relating to, 36
stakeholders relating to, 35

rewards, organizational culture, 103
rubrics, 51–53, 55, 120–21

scholar-practitioners, professional
    development for, 76, 99, 101
  evolutions in, 100
  learning and pedagogy relating
      to, 100
  plans for, 100
Schroeder, Charles, 108
Schwartz, Barry, 10
self-awareness, 47–48, 50, 120
sequencing. *See* developmentally
    sequenced learning
Sexual Violence Prevention month,
    61
shared goals, 34–35
shared student learning-focused
    language, 15
"Shifting to Curricular Approaches
    to Learning Beyond the
    Classroom" (Kerr et al.), xiv
shifts, in organizational culture,
    102–3
Skyfactor Benchmark surveys, 16
Small Teaching (Lang), 77
social inequities, 85
social justice-oriented learning, 86,
    88
socially constructed knowledge,
    learning, and pedagogy, 84
societal expectations, of higher
    education, 2
sphere of influence, 106–7
stakeholders
  engagement of, 35, 36, 44, 54,
      130
  information to, 45, 51, 63, 65,
      70, 104
status quo challenge, 20–21

strategic planning, 112
strategies, 8
  for leadership, 109–12
  learning aims and, 23, 27–28
  for learning outcomes, 50, 122
strategy-level learning outcomes, 28,
    65–66
structural frame of organizations,
    129–30
student administration, 6
student affairs, 1–4, 101
  evolution of, 5–6
  identity development relating to,
      5
  intersectionality relating to, 5
student affairs educators
  contributions of, 2, 5–6
  curricular approach of, 19–20
  informed decisions of, 3
  learning aims relating to, 39–40
  obligations of, 1, 55
student affairs roles, as educators
  myths about, 75
  pedagogies relating to, 75–76
  resources for, 75–76
  rethinking roles of, 74–76
  understanding of, 74
student learning, 5, 6, 20–21
  centering of, 76
  curricular approach to, xv,
      22–24, 23, 29–30, 36–37,
      115
  educational strategies for, 23,
      28–30, 37
  with paradigm shift, 14–15
student learning beyond classroom,
    1–2, 73
  conclusion to, 95
  learning process, 80–83
  neuroscience of learning, 78–79

pedagogical strategies, 88–95, 128
perspective on knowledge, learning, pedagogy, 84–88
rethinking student affairs roles as educators, 74–76
types of learning, 77–78
what is learning, 76–77
who are learners, 83–84
Student Learning Imperative, 3, 108
students
  development of, 6
  educational needs of, 2–3
  experience value of, 2
  learning process for issues of, 82
  satisfaction of, 8
  services for, 6
  success indicators of, 6
Students will be able to (SWBAT), 49, 66
"The Student Learning Imperative," 5, 20
substance free life, xii
success
  indicators of, 6
  measured, 16–17
  measurement of, 8–9
SWBAT. *See* Students will be able to
symbolic frame of organizations, 131
systems
  accountability, 85
  of power and oppression impact, 84–86

Take Back the Night march, 61
teacher-centric approach, 11
Teaching Across Cultural Strengths (Chavez and Longerbeam), 86

Teaching for Diversity and Social Justice (Adams et al.), 87
teams, 41–43, 59–60, 112
technological tools
  for archeological dig, 43
  utilization of, 93
technology, mobile, 83
themes with educational priority, 44
time management, 10–11
"The Time Has Come to Create Meaning-Making Centers on College Campuses (Nash and Jang), 94
tools
  for assessment plans, 69
  for Divisional Barometer for the Curricular Approach in Student Affairs, 129
  technical, 43, 93
traditional approach, curricular approach *versus*, 3–4, 20, 116
traditional educational approach critique
  communities of practice relating to, 6
  educational aims identification relating to, 7–8
  educator philosophy relating to, 6–7
  lack of focus, 7
  lack of goals and strategies, 8
  lack of intersectionality, 9
  Learning Reconsidered relating to, 6
  pedagogy relating to, 9
  student satisfaction relating to, 8
  success measurement relating to, 8–9
  time management relating to, 10–11

transformative education outcomes, 12
transformative learning, 78

underlying assumptions, organizational culture with, 103, 104

unlearning, 80

vision, institution mission with, 22

Whitt, E. J., 12
worksheet, archeological dig learning aims, 43–44

For Product Safety Concerns and Information please contact our EU
representative GPSR@taylorandfrancis.com
Taylor & Francis Verlag GmbH, Kaufingerstraße 24, 80331 München, Germany

www.ingramcontent.com/pod-product-compliance
Lightning Source LLC
Chambersburg PA
CBHW050639300426
44112CB00012B/1859